A Better Democracy

A Better Democracy

Sixty-Five Million People at the Palais Bourbon

Emilio Dib

Prudent Pigeon Publishing

Copyright © 2013 by Emilio Dib

All rights reserved. No part of this book may be reproduced, stored in a retrieval system, or transmitted without the prior written permission of the author.

The author will usually grant permission, but would like to know who is taking interest in his work.

Prudent Pigeon Publishing
Marseille
France

ISBN: 978-2-9544542-0-7

2 4 6 8 10 9 7 5 3 1

Cover illustration by Johnny Dib

A toi, mon cœur.

Table of Contents

Introduction	1
Legislative Element	7
Discovering Law	13
Proposing Law	17
Debating Law	21
Voting Law	24
Executive Element	29
Elections	30
Interaction of Government & Citizens	38
Council of Presidents	45
Conclusion	49
Appendices	
Deliberation	59
Happiness	75
Morality	83
Cooperation	95
Justice	101
Notes	109
Bibliography	161

Introduction

We are fortunate to live in relatively stable, prosperous, and free societies.[1] Then why write this essay?

As in many other domains of life, perfecting the organization of our community is an endless journey. We can constantly move toward this goal, but never reach it. However, there is merit in examining the status quo, tinkering with it, looking at it from different standpoints, and coming up with one or two ideas that move the discussion forward.

But is there anything worth changing? Can there be concrete improvements, beyond theoretical and philosophical considerations? Haven't we reached the ultimate system of government?

In fact, history seems clearer and more predictable in hindsight.[2] Past events look to us more obvious than they really were.

In the year 100 AD, very few people saw the end of Rome coming. Hardly any contemporaries could have predicted the collapse of one of the largest empires of the ancient world. And the same may be said about Babylon, Pella, Cusco, Avarga[3] and most other centers of civilization.

Take for example an educated thinker living in Europe during the High Middle Ages, when most of the continent was organized by a political system of feudalism and engaged in a game of musical chairs among kingdoms. Let us call our friendly thinker Bernart. If we asked Bernart how he sees the political environment developing in the future, chances are that he would have missed the possibility that republics would eventually come to replace feudalism.

Likewise, we would have had a similar situation if we asked Elizaveta, a fictitious

INTRODUCTION

student of literature living in Moscow at the height of the cold war, about the future of the Soviet Union.

And so today, we probably have a bias in favor of the status quo when we think about the future of democracy.

But let us try to liberate ourselves from this status quo. Let us remember that today's political systems[4] will have evolved in a thousand years, even in a hundred years, and perhaps even in ten years or less.

So change is coming, but in which direction? And will it have a positive impact?

One way to determine whether a political change is positive is to use a simple rule of thumb inspired by Aristotle. According to the teacher of Alexander the Great, the first goal of a political system is to enable the *good life* of its citizens.[5]

Aristotle's concept of the good life may be seen to comprise the notions of happiness, prosperity, health, safety… or the conditions that empower us to inquire and create.[6]

Based on this, we will try to look at our current institutions with a critical eye and consider ways in which they may be tweaked in order to increase the good life of the people. The modest ideas that we arrive at, or stumble upon, will hopefully contribute to the larger discussion surrounding the constant evolution of our society.

> "In our own day, verdicts are given, deliberations are carried on, and decisions are arrived at by people acting together."

This statement may sound to some like utopia or a goal to be realized in the distant future. Indeed, how wonderful it must be for all people living in a democracy to sit together, think about problems, debate various courses of action, and collectively arrive at solutions.

But the same Aristotle wrote those words about 2,400 years ago.[7] Of course, we are not advocating a Back-to-the-Future-style scenario because the entire context has changed.

INTRODUCTION

The size of our societies has grown drastically[8] and the circle of people who count as citizens has been enlarged.[9]

But is representative democracy inescapable?[10] Can there be a smarter legislative process that removes the intermediaries and puts the citizens back at the heart of lawmaking?

Likewise, the executive branch of our modern democracies can be looked at through a critical lens.

Today's executive cycle peaks at the time of elections, during campaigning and the actual vote. From that point forward, the citizens seem removed from the process.

And once crowned, the executive strays away from their election promises so routinely that dedicated websites specialized in listing broken promises have cropped up around the world.

But can there be a way to maintain a stronger link between electoral programs and actual policy?[11] Can we make the executive more accountable to the people?

In this work, we do not aim to tear down our current institutions, but to strengthen them. Our aim is for the people to become more effective owners of the political system.

Indeed modern democracies, at times, appear to disempower citizens, leaving them with fake choices and turning them into cynics. And this shows up in low election turnouts and in the polarization of voters around moral values,[12] instead of debating actions, trade-offs, and their consequences for society.

We hope that all this tinkering with our institutions will generate a few humble, yet concrete ideas—instead of a grand theory—that make our democracies more robust.[13]

Legislative Element

The essence of democracy resides in the rule of the people and in equality before the law. To move toward this purpose, we suggest a system of direct democracy in which all citizens are invited to become legislators without the need for intermediaries.[1]

In it, the body of citizens forms the legislative institution. The people collectively hold the power of lawmaking: they propose, debate, and vote on law.

- Proposing law: Citizens are invited to propose legislation, in the form of a bill.
- Debating law: Bills are then debated among willing citizens. They may be

complemented, forming projects of law.
- Voting on law: When enough citizens sponsor a project of law, it goes to vote and becomes law.

Yet can this goal of direct democracy be achieved? Perhaps it can if we take advantage of the technological progress of the last few decades,[2] and build a dedicated platform on top of a secure computer network. This platform may be made out of four environments.

1. Discover: where law is published and can be browsed and searched.
2. Propose: where people propose new law.
3. Debate: in which deliberation is held around bills.
4. Vote: where citizens vote on law.

LEGISLATIVE ELEMENT

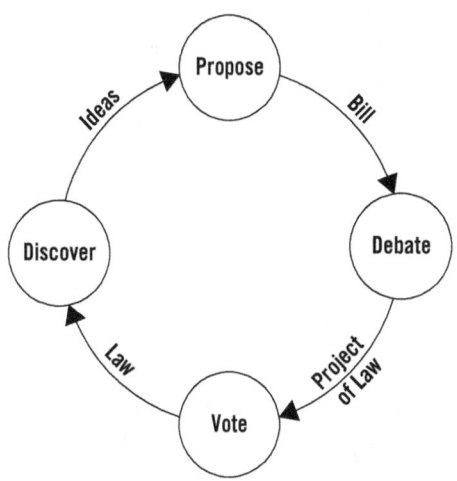

But before describing the workings of such a system, one can already hear the objections. The first one being that the mass of the people is neither willing nor capable of such a task. Let us consider this doubt, which basically breaks down to: know-how, motivation and availability.

Know-how: In representative democracies, we delegate our legislative powers to members of parliament. But know-how is a prerequisite for effective delegation.[3] Therefore, if we consider our current representative democracies to be democratic, then we already have this know-how. Consequently, this argument cannot be raised against a direct democracy without it being raised against the status quo.

Furthermore, we maintain that the collective wisdom is higher than the sum of individual knowledge. Even when all individuals do not have equal skills in a particular field,[4] the group of citizens contains within it the best possible knowledge in all fields;[5] certainly more so than any group of members of parliament.[6]

Motivation: In the knowledge realm, motivation can be driven by autonomy, mastery, and purpose as Daniel Pink has argued.[7] But autonomy, mastery, and purpose are at the heart of the proposed legislative process.[8]

In the political system that is described here, individuals are free to participate, and consciously express their views (autonomy). They feel encouraged to deepen their

LEGISLATIVE ELEMENT

knowledge, and to excel in the topics they contribute to (mastery). And they have a sense of belonging, and contribute to something that is larger than oneself (purpose).

Availability: The free time argument usually goes along the following lines. We need members of parliament (full-time professionals) to do the legislative job on our behalf because we do not have enough time to do it ourselves.

But when one looks into the matter, the data seems to suggest a different conclusion. According to a number of statistics,[9] the average day contains as much as 20% of free time. This *free time* includes community work and social interaction as well as recreation and leisure, so it would be unfair to say that we do nothing of as much as 5 hours of every day.

However, what if we could, on average, use 1% to 2% of our individual free time to propose, debate, and decide on topics that matter to us? That would amount to more than 25 hours per person and per year.[10] And it is only fair to assume that most of us will spend at least some time on the topics that are closest to our hearts.[11] Furthermore, 25 hours per person amount to about 1.25 billion hours for the adult population of a country about the size of France. That is about one thousand times more than what members of parliament and senators put in, assuming that they dedicate their full working time to their legislative duties.[12]

Therefore, the short answer to the three counter-arguments is that a direct participation of citizens brings more know-how and more time to solve the challenges of our countries, with the added benefit of more engaged citizens.

The following paragraphs discuss a number of ways[13] to discover, propose, debate, and vote on law.

LEGISLATIVE ELEMENT

Discovering Law

Power requires knowledge.[14] Therefore, the first step in empowering people to become legislators is to make law accessible, which means: easily discoverable and understandable.

In addition to making law searchable,[15] this can be accomplished in two ways: simplification, and training.[16] Gradually, a majority of citizens ought to achieve a level of proficiency in law comparable to newly elected members of parliament.

Simplification. To simplify law we can reduce its volume.

At the dawn of this century, France had about 9,000 laws and 120,000 decrees. Since then, 70 laws and 1,500 decrees have been added each year, on average.[17] The current French civil law is made of more than 60 volumes of code. It can probably be streamlined to less than 10.[18]

On top of that, the global volume of law can be reduced by observing rules of judicial hygiene, such as:

1. Merging related laws that deal with the same topic from different viewpoints,
2. Replacing old laws by the new ones whenever an amendment is adopted,[19]
3. Regularly reviewing and simplifying law to ensure that it is written clearly,
4. And repealing law that dictates micro-behaviors, as much as possible.

Montesquieu put it best when he wrote: "we should not do with law what we can do through mores."[20] We should leave some space for common sense and refrain from codifying every aspect of our lives. In fact, the main purpose of law is *to set boundaries protecting an open field of freedom, and not to intercede in all disputes* according to Philip Howard.[21] Howard also gives us the application handbook of this elegant idea: *to rebuild boundaries of freedom, two changes*

LEGISLATIVE ELEMENT

are essential: simplify the law, and restore the authority to judges to apply it.

Simplification of law—without excess[22]—is not only possible; it is a key to a thriving democracy. It will become less and less tolerated in our age of information that so many people have such a little grasp of the overwhelming volume of law.

Many active citizens with an idea to move the society forward quickly find themselves drowned in an interlaced legislation in which many laws are 100 pages long, and include more than 100 articles. On top of that, many articles consist of references and amendments to other law. So that in order to understand a simple piece of legislation, one has to go back and read all the related law going back decades, sometimes even centuries.[23]

Training. Training is the second prerequisite, in addition to simplification, to make law accessible to most citizens.

Throughout our life we learn to read,

which allows us to gain access to the vast human knowledge. We learn to write, which allows us to contribute to this knowledge. We learn some math, which is a powerful vocabulary for ideas. We learn a craft, which allows us to become talented workers... Then it is only logical that we learn about our laws if we want to become good citizens.

After all, the Aristotelian adage *nobody is supposed to be ignorant of the law* is very useful to prevent criminals from pleading their innocence on the basis of ignorance. We think that this saying should also be at work for all well-meaning individuals. Let us make it a goal of our modern societies that a majority of citizens become acquainted with the workings and content of law.[24]

To achieve this, children could have their first contact with the legislative and judiciary systems as of middle school. From there, they can gradually learn about the workings and content of law, all the way to high school and university. Then during their adult lives, people may attend yearly sessions to refresh

LEGISLATIVE ELEMENT

their knowledge and get acquainted with new law.[25]

In our daily lives, we must feel confident that if we are acting reasonably, we will not be liable to lawsuits. Furthermore, we must have a sense of legal literacy allowing us to undertake projects, start businesses, found associations, build, create, and discover. Law must enable us and expand our horizons, not hinder us.

In Howard's words, *more than just knowing the law, understanding it brings trust in it; and trust in law is an essential condition of freedom.*

Proposing Law

To discuss how law is proposed, let us follow Lisa, a fictitious schoolteacher and young mom. Lisa has a number of ideas that she would like to share with her fellow citizens. She thinks that those ideas may benefit the community, and she would like to discuss them with others and learn from their reactions.

Lisa is well armed for this endeavor. Like the majority of her fellow citizens, she knows how the legal system works. She has always had a curious mind and has already attended discussion sessions with judges from her community. Furthermore, having contributed to a recent debate on a bill that went on to become law, she is confident that she too has what it takes to share her views with others.

Lisa is keen to have speed limits reduced to 30 km/h[26] within cities for several reasons: more security, a more fluid circulation, less fuel consumption and air pollution, and less noise pollution. She is convinced that this measure would have a minimal effect on travel time since the average vehicle speed within cities is between 10 and 25 km/h anyway, with peaks of 50 km/h.[27]

In fact, Lisa has noticed that traffic noise

LEGISLATIVE ELEMENT

is much lower next to her school (which is located in a 30 km/h zone). She feels that pedestrians, bicycles, and cars move around more harmoniously there. So she researched this topic and found that the city of Graz in Austria has implemented a 30 km/h speed limit with positive results.

Lisa logs-in to the proposal environment using her real identity.[28] She enters a search query for *speed limit within cities*. And sure enough, one of the first results that she gets is from the traffic code, which specifies the current speed limit at 50 km/h. Lisa reads the law and clicks to amend it. She replaces 50 km/h with 30 km/h and goes on to comment her change. She cites the goals of this change (security, fluidity, pollution), the example and results of Graz, and invites her fellow citizens to give feedback.

In the following months, a group of university professors complements Lisa's arguments with results from their research on traffic fluidity. An association fighting against road accidents supports her proposal with data showing the relation between vehicle speed and traffic-related deaths. Engineers working for a car manufacturer weigh in with the data on reduced fuel consumption. And a group of civil servants suggests that the implementation be progressive in order to measure the results and facilitate the change.

After months of discussion, Lisa's proposal was starting to look solid and attract attention. People were starting to sponsor it.[29] Eventually, Lisa's proposal for a reduced speed limit garners the endorsement of 1/1000 of eligible citizens[30] and it becomes a bill.

So Lisa, an ordinary citizen with an idea, can easily propose a new law or an amendment to existing law.[31] But the executive branch of government may also propose law, which then follows the exact same path as Lisa's proposal.[32]

The group of citizens, as an institution, has the legislative power in hand.[33]

LEGISLATIVE ELEMENT

Debating Law

When enough citizens have sponsored a proposal, it moves to the next stage in the process: debate. Bills in the debate environment are more mature and have more visibility than proposals. They attract a higher level of interest and scrutiny from citizens, and groups of people hold lively deliberations around each bill.*

Lisa's bill is now subjected to a national debate. During this phase, willing citizens weigh in on the bill with arguments for their endorsement or opposition. Citizens may also react to the arguments of one another—within the rules of good conduct. So that after several months of public deliberation:

- Lisa has incorporated a number of key amendments to her bill (such

---

* See Appendix A for more on Deliberation

as the possibility for cities to exceptionally set higher speed limits on major arteries).
- The arguments in favor and against her bill have reached a high level of quality (in particular, a notorious academic made the top opposing argument while a bus driver made the most insightful supporting argument).[34]

During months of discussion, the speed limit bill is subjected to a solid deliberation and gains visibility and the endorsement of one per cent of eligible citizens.[35] Lisa becomes satisfied with her final draft and decides to put it to vote.[36] The bill now becomes a project of law.

The debate environment is a collection of bills—like Lisa's—at different stages of maturity. And a civic debate is held around each of those bills: A few will get amended and move on to the voting stage while others will be

LEGISLATIVE ELEMENT

discarded or sent back to the proposal stage to mature. In all cases, these ideas contribute to elevating the political discussion.

At any given time, not all citizens would be debating all the proposed bills. This may depend on each person's centers of interest and character, and whether they feel linked to the issue at hand. In addition, some citizens might be more active, on average, than others in the legislative process. And groups of people will naturally form around causes and then disassemble.

The whole thing will hopefully be organic. It would foster the engagement of individuals within the larger community and turn everyone who wishes to into an owner of the body of law.

We hope that such a process, in which people assemble around topics and where ideas flow freely and build on one another, has the potential to enable creative improvements to our society and clever solutions to the problems we face.

A BETTER DEMOCRACY

In the words of John Milton:

> "All opinions, yea errors, known, read, and collated, are of main service and assistance towards the speedy attainment of what is truest."[37]

Voting Law

Let us now go back to our cheerful teacher, who has already become a local hero at her school.

Lisa's project of law is now in the voting stage. It is advertised as such for a few weeks in order to allow it to gain more visibility and a wider involvement from the general population.[38]

Following that period, the project is put up for vote for another few weeks. At the end of the voting period, if the majority of voters approve it, the project becomes law.[39]

LEGISLATIVE ELEMENT

The following is a (fictitious) extract of the voting record on Lisa's proposal.

[...]

AABJ-54092748[40]   Against
AACG-42891648   In favor
ABTF-48372610   In favor
AEMG-37809124   Against
ANBV-28187249   Blank
AOUI-35692712   In favor
ABWQ-85721701   Blank
ADSE-56739281   Against
ARED-47302798   Against
AFTY-57836209   In favor

[…]

- Number of votes in favor:
  5 502 073, or 54.96% of the votes
- Number of votes against:
  4 010 301, or 40.06% of the votes

A BETTER DEMOCRACY

- Number of blank votes:
  498 245, or 4.97% of the votes

Let us all congratulate Lisa whose project has gained a majority of the vote and has now become law.

Following this long but intense adventure, Lisa feels that she is a more accomplished citizen. She has gained a strong sense of connection with her community. And she intends to renew her initiative as she has other ideas to share.

At any given time, several projects of law are in the process of votation.[41] Furthermore, the ideas that are debated become discussion topics within society. In turn, they inspire other Lisas, with different ideas, to come forward and share their thoughts—thereby completing the legislative cycle.[42]

As she advances through the legislative process, Lisa—as well as all those who dedicated time and effort to comment, sponsor,

LEGISLATIVE ELEMENT

deliberate and vote—is awarded medals which reward her engagement as a citizen and as a legislator.

These symbols have little material value, but a great moral one. People are proud to display them (for example on their resumes) because they testify to their sense of engagement and to their perseverance.[43] Such medals say to the community: *I am involved. I am curious and take interest in the world around me, and I transform my thoughts into action. I am part of something larger than myself.*[44]

In the end, such a system of direct democracy seems to please the preferences of both liberals and conservatives.

In fact, the ideas of those leaning to the left are usually built on the principles of liberty, equality, and social justice.[45] And this sentiment is echoed here.

In the same time, those leaning to the right usually favor some *laissez-faire*,[46] a reduction of government intervention, and a certain reliance on tested and proven methods. And those values are also defended here since the suggested changes give more power to the people, and favor trial-and-error instead of a grand theory of social engineering.

Executive Element

Now that the people *are* the legislature, can we envisage an improved executive?

Under the principle of separation of powers, the three branches of government have complementary responsibilities. While the legislative branch is responsible for enacting law and the judiciary branch for interpreting it, the executive branch of government executes the law. And all three act in order to move the good life of the people forward.

As such, we may expect a better executive to be more mindful of the best interest of the people and, in the same time, to become more accountable to them. But can this be achieved? Let us look at this question from the standpoints of the elections and the interaction of government and citizens.

Elections

In the proposed system, the people choose among electoral programs in order to set the policy of the executive institution. Teams of aspiring candidates write those programs. They are concise documents that present policy goals in measurable and timely terms.[1] In other words, each program is a specific agenda to advance the good life of the people.

Programs reflect their authors' views. Naturally, different teams may choose to focus on different topics. They may commit to a few or several objectives—such as a happiness index (experienced *and* remembered),[*] GDP growth, unemployment statistics, crime rates, health metrics, income equality, pollution

---

[*] See Appendix B for more on Happiness

EXECUTIVE ELEMENT

measurements, etc.

Any group of determined individuals may propose a program, provided they have actively contributed to the legislative process.[2] If the program is endorsed by 5% of eligible citizens,[3] it goes on to the voting stage. And the aspiring teams who make it this far become candidates to form the council of ministers.

To describe how the elections are conducted, let us look at another fictitious character.

> Chris is a happily married father of three who loves to ski and play tennis. He is a successful entrepreneur and someone who is well appreciated for his good character and for his many contributions to the community.
>
> Chris cares deeply for his country. He regularly takes part in legislative debates and has already proposed a number of bills, nine of which went on to become law.
>
> A bunch of friends manage to convince Chris that he has what it takes to run for

office and become the country's next prime minister. Therefore, after much thought, he assembles a team of his most trusted, skilled and committed connections and together, they produce the first draft of an electoral program.

In the following months, they gradually fine-tune their proposals as they share them with an ever-increasing circle of people. Support for their program grows slowly at first, but expands rapidly soon thereafter.

This is when Chris and his team decide that the project is worth pursuing further. They formally announce their candidature and, soon afterwards, close to 3 million people endorse their program. *(Let us call it program C.)* This means that they are now one of five teams competing to lead the executive branch of government.

Throughout this process, deliberation around the proposed programs is convened among citizens. In addition, when the results of the endorsement are announced, and the

EXECUTIVE ELEMENT

competing teams formally step forward, question-and-answer sessions are held between the people and the candidates.[4]

At this point, elections are conducted using a ranked voting method.[5] In such a system, each voter ranks the programs in order of preference. If, as in this case, 5 programs are endorsed, voters may rank them from 1 to 5.

In the first tally of votes, the first preference of each voter is counted. If a program holds an absolute majority, it wins. Otherwise, the program that holds the fewest preferences is eliminated and the ballots assigned to it are redistributed to the remaining programs based on their next preference. This process is repeated until one program achieves the majority of votes. At which point it is considered to reflect the general will.[6]

As an example, let us consider a fabricated voter called Alice. Following her participation in Q&A sessions with the candidates, and after careful consideration of the proposed executive goals, Alice decides to rank the programs as follows:

- Program A 3
- Program B 1 (most preferred)
- Program C 4[7]
- Program D 2
- Program E 5 (least preferred)

At the voting closure, the count of the first preferences of all voters gives the following results:

- Program A 17%
- Program B 14%
- Program C 24%
- Program D 26%
- Program E 19%

None of the programs gathers an absolute majority of the vote. But since program B has the least first preferences, it is eliminated and its ballots are redistributed to the other programs according to their second

EXECUTIVE ELEMENT

preference. So Alice's vote now goes to program D, since that is her next preference.

Second count:

- Program A   19%
- Program B   -
- Program C   33%
- Program D   28%
- Program E   20%

And this is repeated until one of the programs achieves more than 50% of the vote.

Third count:

- Program A   -
- Program B   -
- Program C   42%
- Program D   33%
- Program E   25%

In such a system, every citizens gets to vote only once and they each have one effective voice. But since they provide a ranking, their voice may go to one or the other program according to their order of preference.

Ranked voting methods reduce tactical voting.[8] They allow more plurality in opinions; thereby fostering a more nuanced political landscape instead of binary moral stands.[9]

Fourth count:

- Program A   -
- Program B   -
- Program C   54%
- Program D   46%
- Program E   -

With the majority of the vote, program C is selected!

Let us all congratulate Chris and his team for winning the elections, and becoming the new prime minister and cabinet

EXECUTIVE ELEMENT

> members. Chris has managed to assemble a team that has won the confidence of his countrymen. And together, they have constructed a program that met the approval of their fellow citizens.[10]

When the count is completed, the program that gathers the absolute majority of votes emerges as the executive's roadmap. Moreover, the team that proposed this program is appointed to conduct the government's policy on behalf of the people.[11]

From this point on, the winning program becomes a moral contract between the elected executive and the people, as in Rousseau's social pact.[12] In addition, since it is a distinct and mandatory part of the electoral process, the contenders avoid making contradictory promises that appeal to separate groups of voters.

That is because the executive branch is expected to honor its promises.

A BETTER DEMOCRACY

Interaction of Government and Citizens

Through the elections, the people express their approval of the executive policy as well as their confidence in the executive team. But those two intents are not indefinite. Therefore, the body of citizens is invited to renew its trust on a yearly basis.

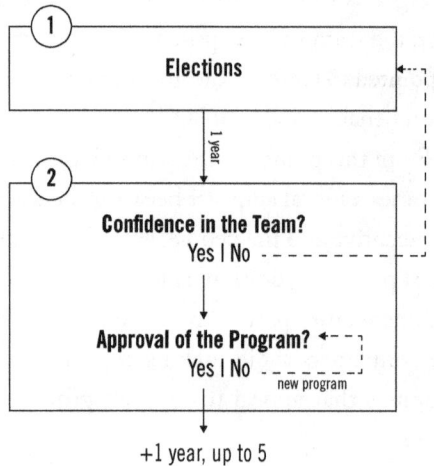

1. Elections are held to choose a Team and its Program
2. A year later, two votes are conducted: First, a vote of Confidence in the Team; Second, a vote of Approval of the Program. This is repeated yearly up to 5 years, and then new Elections are held.

EXECUTIVE ELEMENT

If, a year into the executive's term, the people's confidence in the team is lost, then new elections are conducted. Otherwise, when confidence is confirmed, if the people still approve the program, the executive's term is renewed for an additional year. Alternatively, the executive team is invited to amend its program.[13] And in all cases, general elections are held five years into the mandate.

This process is comparable to a number of parliamentary democracies in which the parliament is invited to express its trust in the government and holds a yearly vote on the government's proposed budget.

To illustrate this further, let us turn back to our friendly prime minister.

> A year after the elections, Chris and his team believe that they have done a very decent job. But what do the people think?
>
> The body of citizens is invited to assess the executive's performance a year into their term. This is done in two successive votes.

First, the people are called to express their continued confidence in the executive team. In this case, they give Chris and his cabinet a firm majority of the confidence vote; which comes as a humbling reward for the team's exemplary conduct of the country's business.

Second, the people are called to express their continued approval of the executive program. In this case, they vote against the current policy. In fact, the economic context has changed much in the last year and some of the program's orientations are no longer in line with the people's aspirations.

Chris and his team acknowledge this vote and draft an adjusted executive program[14] that gets approved by the people. Their term is prolonged by an additional year and they go back to conducting the state's policy soon thereafter.

Such an executive process, accompanied by deliberation, enables the continuous engagement of citizens in public life.[15] It allows the

EXECUTIVE ELEMENT

people to further exercise their democratic role by repeatedly assessing their country's policy and the individuals who are conducting it—all while mitigating the effects of the illusion of foresight.[16]

By the same token, it discourages potential contenders for public office from promising goals that they cannot achieve. And this is consistent with such views as those of Locke, Popper, or Rawls.[17]

Moreover, although at any given moment the country is set on a clear path, this political system is frankly empirical.[18] It allows for mistakes to be made[19] and forecasts to be wrong, and it acknowledges political complexity in general.[20]

At its heart, such a process is based on trial-and-error and the continuous fine-tuning of the public agenda.

Furthermore, if we go back to the elections, the reasons for this approach become even clearer. In the proposed system, elections are held to choose one of several teams who propose distinct policy goals in their respective programs.

Those programs deal with the *what*, not the *how*. That is, they present measurable results to be achieved and not the precise actions in order to achieve them. The latter are up to the elected executive, who is granted the mandate to carry out public policy—the executive makes all the necessary policy decisions, within the legal framework that is defined by the legislature.

The citizens, through lawmaking, define the rules that everyone must respect, the people *and* the government. But they do not define the day-to-day actions of the government.[21]

To illustrate, and answer a recurring question, let us take the difficult case of war. If, during the executive's mandate, an external aggressor attacks the nation, and if the law permits a direct military retaliation in the case of aggression, then the executive does not need to wait for an additional vote from the people in order to retaliate.

EXECUTIVE ELEMENT

In this case as in all others, the executive's duty is to *execute* the law—and to do it justly. But, within those two constraints, they use their best judgment in conducting the governmental policy.

At this point, we can start seeing the larger benefits from a continuous citizen engagement in public life.[22] Through the elections, the people choose quantifiable policy goals and a competent team to carry them out. They reassess, yearly, the continued validity of the program and the performance of the team. And they re-express, yearly as well, their agreement with the conduct of policy and their confidence in the executive team who is leading it.

In fact, in the proposed system the executive power is more united, and more decisive than in our modern democracies. In addition, it is more democratic. The proposed executive is unified in carrying out a clear roadmap and it has a stronger mandate to execute it. Nevertheless, it must do so after a careful and recurrent citizen validation of the program and within a legal framework that is sanctioned by the people.

With regard to the powers vested in the executive branch of government, our current democracies cope well with human failings and limit corruption with good success.[23] And we think that we should go even further.

In the proposed democracy, public officials should be held to higher standards—more responsibilities leading to more accountability, not more immunity.[24] Furthermore, our political environment should be distinctly honest[25] and transparent.[26]

> Those who engage in public life ought to exhibit justice and courage, culture and education,[27] they should be guardians of the laws and institutions, demonstrate a love of knowledge and learning, be truthful and temperate, curious, sociable and experienced.[28]

EXECUTIVE ELEMENT

Aristotle and Plato set the bar really high. And we dream that one day public affairs will be conducted with such virtue.*

Meanwhile, we hope that the notions which have been considered up to now would encourage statesmen to surround themselves by more scientists, researchers, and thinkers and less donors, lobbyists, and celebrities—thereby continuing the march toward the good life of the people.[29]

Council of Presidents

To further strengthen public participation, the position of head of state may be held by a collegial council of 5 people. Its members are selected at random from a pool of qualified citizens. And all those who have made decisive contributions[30] to the legislative process are candidates, by default, for this position.

---

* See Appendix C on Morality

A yearly allotment is conducted to renew three of the five *presidents*, so that the council is entirely renewed every two years.[31] Of course, the selected candidates may accept or refuse the appointment.

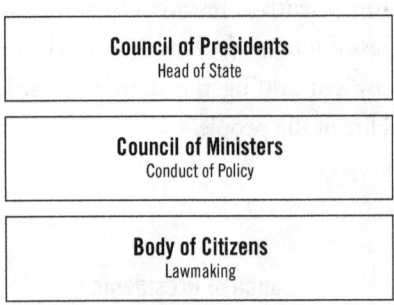

The role of head of state is largely symbolic.[32] It embodies the spirit of the republic[33] and acts as a public representative of the state. The 5-member council partakes in formal events and diplomatic protocols. It may have a supervisory role, observing the actions of the executive.

Democracy does not necessarily imply

EXECUTIVE ELEMENT

elections. In the Athenian Democracy, public officials were primarily selected by allotment, and random selection was considered a principal characteristic of democracy.[34] Some, like Montesquieu, go even further by claiming: "the suffrage by lot is natural to democracy, as that by choice is to aristocracy."[35]

In fact, random selection is essentially democratic since all qualified citizens have equal chances of being appointed. Over the long run, everyone is represented.

Consider the change in mindset when, following the implementation of such a presidential council, more and more citizens may be able to say *one of my ancestors was president*. And everyone can realize that *I too may one day accede to the highest position that the state has to offer*.

Conclusion

The republic will always remain more a work in progress than a set of institutions.¹ As such, we persist in our optimism that the ideas presented in this work, however basic, may one day contribute to the ongoing project of building our democracy.²

There is a case to be made for systems that encourage collective efforts toward a better society—away from radical moral stands and ideology. And we think that the direct democracy that is described in these pages may contribute to this goal.³

In fact, such a system has the potential to empower groups of talented people to engage around positive ideas; instead of the everlasting binary confrontations between government and opposition.

However, there are objections to such a democracy and they are worth considering.

> "You are putting too much trust in the good intentions of people and in their willingness to behave constructively," our critics may tell us. "You are assuming too easily that individuals will spontaneously start working for the sake of their community."

The main criticism to any participative democracy—and this one in particular—seems to revolve around people's inner motives. But we are not making any assumptions about human nature.

It does not matter much, in this work, whether people are essentially altruistic and benevolent or individualistic and self-interested.[4] In the second case, public interest would still be advanced as individuals work to promote their egoistic causes; in a similar

CONCLUSION

manner to merchants working to further their interests, as described by Adam Smith, and to the prisoners in Albert Tucker's dilemma.[5]

So human nature may lie on either side of those two cartoonish extremes, or anywhere in between, without much incidence on the proposed democracy.

Furthermore, such objections cannot be raised against the proposed system without them being raised against the status quo. If, for example, people are indeed fundamentally selfish, then members of parliament and ministers are selfish as well. So how come we accept them as our rulers in current democracies?

Another criticism we hear relates to responsibility—or rather the dilution thereof.

> "If the citizens collectively establish the laws of the land, then responsibility for a potentially bad law is distributed onto a large number of people," our critics may say. "Therefore, each individual experiences

a very small part of responsibility. And, liberated from that weight, the people start passing bad laws."

"Conversely," according to our critics, "the benefit of having a few representatives take care of lawmaking is that they each carry a greater responsibility over their shoulders. And thanks to this, members of parliament are able to overcome their shady instincts and make better law than the mass of the people."

Our critics then propose an interesting thought experiment to illustrate this point. "Take the basic example of taxation laws," they tell us. "The majority of citizens would probably vote to reduce, or even repeal taxes. And this would lead to the collapse of government. But whose fault would that be? What you're proposing is a charming democracy in which no one can be blamed for bad law."

This hypothesis is different from the previous one. In addition to addressing human

CONCLUSION

nature at the level of the individual, it proposes that human behavior may change as the individual goes from being alone to being part of a larger group.

It is a compelling counter argument. Unfortunately, a similar criticism—of little *experienced responsibility*[6]—may again be raised against the status quo. In fact, there are more than a few examples of bad law that was passed by very smart representatives.[7]

But you know what? This situation is perhaps not as dramatic as it may seem.[8] That is because our societies learn from their mistakes. They reiterate and improve.[9]

Accordingly, one can easily imagine a similar corrective process taking place in the proposed system. The citizens would continuously reiterate and improve law. Gradually, as they feel more empowered, they become more responsible.[10]

Furthermore, the people have ample reason to feel the weight of responsibility, perhaps even more so than representatives. At the end of the day, it is citizens who bear the cost of unjust law, either directly or indirectly.

In the example of taxes, either the people directly pay the price of the collapse of government (no more public schools and hospitals), or their children and grandchildren will.[11]

So the counter-argument is very interesting. But it does not seem to spare the status quo. Furthermore, since it is the people who pay the bill, they may even become more (not less) responsible lawmakers. And this very behavior—of an increase in experienced responsibility—has been measured by a number of studies.[12]

So let them have this *charming democracy!*

Few have trouble acknowledging the effectiveness of deliberation in a small team.[13] Within groups of a few to a few dozen, we routinely decide together which movie to watch, the planned conference's agenda, or the location of the next big family reunion.

CONCLUSION

In fact, for much of our existence as humans, we have lived in bands and tribes and arrived at decisions collectively.[14] And perhaps that is why direct democracy seems to make us happier.[15]

Then our communities grew in size, and this created the need for intermediaries.[16] But our communities are becoming small again. Thanks to communication technologies, we are only a few steps—or a few clicks—away from almost anyone in the world. We now routinely participate in video-conferences across time zones and in common interest forums across continents.[17] So it only seems natural, not to mention much more efficient, that the number of intermediaries will decrease again—including in politics. And this is a favorable environment for the emergence of cooperation.* However, to see it, we need to liberate ourselves from the weight of the status quo.[18]

In practice, the proposed system may

---

* See Appendix D for more on Cooperation

either generate a wiki-democracy in which most people contribute to public life or a situation similar to the status quo wherein a limited number of active citizens dominate much of the public discourse—or perhaps an intermediary, hybrid situation.[19]

The key philosophical difference is that the barrier to entry becomes drastically lowered compared to the current systems,[20] to the benefit of society.*

We think that this is a significant step toward a better democracy.

---

* Appendix E discusses how this upholds Justice.

The dogmas of the quiet past are inadequate to the stormy present. The occasion is piled high with difficulty, and we must rise—with the occasion. As our case is new, so we must think anew, and act anew.

Fellow-citizens, we cannot escape history.

Abraham Lincoln, *Message to Congress*

Appendix A

Deliberation

It may not surprise the reader that deliberation among tens or even hundreds of million of individuals is not very practicable as such. At best, it may lead to a limited number of 'star orators' monopolizing the discussion— at worse, to complete chaos. And there is science beneath this common intuition. This appendix explores some of this science. It is mainly based on the work of James Fishkin as discussed in his *When the People Speak*.

In order to encourage thoughtful citizen deliberation in the proposed democracy, people are assembled in groups—particularly in the proposal and debate environments.

So when citizens like Lisa want to propose new bills, they do it on a national, community-wide, level. Then, still on a national level, they nurture their proposal through the debate and up to the final vote. But when other citizens connect to the platform to explore proposals and give their opinion, they do so from within their group. This means that they debate primarily with members of their own group.

In fact, each citizen is randomly assigned to a group of 500+ individuals. These groups are stable, which means that existing members remain in the group, as new ones are added. And an algorithm automatically enlarges the group by admitting new members (such as citizens who reach maturity), in order to ensure a minimum level of activity within each group. Conversely, if the activity of a group peaks in a given period, members may be randomly assigned to smaller subgroups of sufficiently limited size, to allow for more effective deliberation.

People debate mainly with members of their own group. However, they may reference opinions and research from other groups

APPENDIX A

as well. And this allows for continuity in the arguments throughout the community and for considerations to build on one another.

In addition to contributing to the emergence of cooperation,* such an organization happens to satisfy Fishkin's three democratic core values of *political equality, deliberation* and *participation*, which form the trilemma described in his *When the People Speak*.

It does so, in particular, by using random sampling to form the groups, by encouraging thoughtful deliberation within each group, and by extending political engagement to all willing citizens.

The following is a brief description of how Political equality, Deliberation, and Participation may be achieved in the proposed democracy.

Political Equality. According to Fishkin, the

---

* See Appendix D for more on Cooperation

root notion of political equality is the equal consideration of political preferences. Everyone's preferences need to count the same.

In the proposed organization, this is achieved through random sampling and equal counting of votes on a national level, and through the equal opportunity for all to participate.

Random sampling is fundamentally equal as none is favored in their belonging to a given group—we are all equidistant from the dice. Counting the votes nationally means that each citizen is given an equal likelihood of being the decisive voter. Furthermore, the equal opportunity of all to participate is achieved under the thin assumptions of near-full literacy and access—all citizens should know how to read and write and all should have access to the public platform.

Taken together, these characteristics lower the barrier to entry so that everyone may be heard equally and that everyone's preferences count the same.

Moreover, in order for political equality to

APPENDIX A

be better achieved, we need thoughtful deliberation—which takes us to the second value.

Deliberation. The proposed organization seems to fulfill Fishkin's five conditions for thoughtful deliberation:

1. *Information:* citizens have access to reasonably accurate information that they believe to be relevant to the issue.

   As in Lisa's example, the legislative system may be designed so that citizens contribute relevant and sourced information to a common repository. This information is then vetted by all and ranked automatically, making it easily accessible to everyone.

2. *Substantive balance:* arguments offered by one side or from one perspective are answered by considerations offered by those holding other perspectives.

As in Lisa's example, arguments build on one another and opposing views are encouraged within each group. An organic list of the top supporting and opposing arguments is also made available to the whole community. This list continues to evolve with the general discussion; it is frozen one day prior to the vote.

3   *Diversity:* the major positions in the public are represented by participants in the discussion.

In the proposed system, the groups are formed by random sampling (similarly to Fishkin's Deliberative Polls). This seems to offer a scientific means of representing the diversity of viewpoints in the population at large within each group.

This criterion is further satisfied by the fact that the general population is invited to participate in the legislative

APPENDIX A

deliberation (when we look at all the groups). And members of one group may reference arguments and viewpoints from other groups.

4 *Conscientiousness:* participants sincerely weigh the merits of the arguments.

As it is set up, the proposed system seems to encourage conscientiousness because, similarly to Deliberative Polls, voting is done by secret ballots[*] and in one round. Furthermore, in Fishkin's words, under most institutional designs, *ordinary citizens have less opportunity to bargain and less opportunity to behave strategically than do political elites.* We think this is the case under the proposed institutional design as well.

---

[*] A variant consists of keeping the votes secret until the voter passes away, thereby sheltering her from undue social pressures while encouraging her to cast votes she would be proud of.

5. *Equal consideration:* arguments offered by all participants are considered on the merits regardless of which participants offer them.

We will again follow Fishkin's argument here. If any group is deliberating, there will surely be variations in their perceived competence and expertise on the subject at hand. It is very likely the case that even informed citizens use shortcuts and heuristics—such as following the opinion of someone who exhibits knowledge or expertise. But even when all this is admitted, the key is that debating citizens will weigh the merits of competing arguments for themselves. Two experts in the group may hold opposing views with different means-ends relations, and each citizen has to weigh the merits of these opposing arguments. And to the extent they are doing so, they are deliberating.

APPENDIX A

John Stuart Mill seems to promote the value of deliberation when he writes: "If there are any persons who contest a received opinion, or who will do so if law or opinion will let them, let us thank them for it, open our minds to listen to them, and rejoice that there is some one to do for us what we otherwise ought, if we have any regard for either the certainty or the vitality of our convictions, to do with much greater labour for ourselves."

Let us now take a brief look at mass participation, our third core value.

Participation. By which Fishkin means behavior on the part of members of the mass public directed at influencing the formulation, adoption, or implementation of governmental or policy choices.

The proposed democracy seems to favor political participation through universal voting, and through the invitation of all citizens to contribute energy—time, arguments, and votes—to affect public choices.

We think that it has the potential to achieve and unprecedented level of participation—both quantitatively and qualitatively.

The proposed system seems to strike an exceptional balance between political equality, deliberation, and participation. This means that, by its design, the proposed democracy appears to offer an interesting mix of the advantages of mass democracy, mobilized deliberation, and microcosmic deliberation with fewer of their shortcomings.

Consequently, this allows for some convergence between *reflective* opinions (those arising from deliberation and considered judgment) and *reflected* opinions (those mirroring the raw views of the many).

Since more people start effectively deliberating, more and more people start holding reflective opinions on public topics. And since those deliberations, by their spread, inevitably spill into the living room, they

APPENDIX A

start coinciding with the reflected opinions of the many.

In our view, this is a significant step toward a better democracy.

To be sure, the proposed system ought to contain certain shock absorbers and speed reducers that elevate the political discussion and allow for composure and endurance in the public debate.

One such mechanism is the judicial branch of government, which guards the constitution, thereby ensuring the basic conditions of justice. Another is the gradual, step-by-step nature of the legislative process: discovery, proposal, debate, and then vote.

Furthermore, prior to starting debates, we must remember that deliberation is an art, even a craft. It presupposes certain skills and a particular environment.

The skills must be learned, hence the importance of civic education and training. And the context must be that of a safe space in which considerations and proposals are expressed, and ideas are fostered.

As such, by its architecture, the proposed platform must encourage citizens to rebound on the content of the arguments of others. For example, the system may reference the arguments semantically; it may allow searching, tagging, and categorization.

It must minimize *ad hominem* attacks and other logical fallacies as well as hateful comments—by allowing the people to report them as such, prompting removal and warnings, for example.

It is true that those who contribute more actively to their groups choose to do so. This means that, within the open invitation and random-selection of group members, there is an element of self-selection to be more or less active. But this is similar to most other domains of public (and even private) life—individuals routinely self-select to run for elections, to cast their vote, to express their opinion in a debate, etc. In some sense, our

APPENDIX A

liberty depends on it.

To be sure, we may setup one or several control groups per debated bill. Each control group would be formed by strict random sampling with an incentive to participate, and this allows us to achieve a higher level of representativeness within those groups. This would complement the overall system in an interesting manner and allow for a number of useful comparisons.[*]

But in any case, in the proposed system, the refined voice of each person is given an unprecedented weight. And that, in itself, is a strong incentive to participate. In such a democracy, we think that many more citizens would choose to partake in public life. And indeed, over the long run, they probably do.

In the least, there is strong reason to believe that all opinions, if not all individuals, would be present in public deliberations—the pros, the antis, and the agnostics of a given view.

---

[*] By the way, we are proponents of empirical research and data analysis, whenever this makes sense.

A BETTER DEMOCRACY

Under the proposed democracy, the people have more (rational) reason to debate, argument, and vote because the stake is no longer binary (blue vs. red), but a much more nuanced and tangible contribution.

"I can contribute to protecting sea life because I *know* the ocean," a passionate scuba diver may think. "I want to share my experience because this law can still be improved."

In the proposed system, we have reason to pay attention. So in some sense, this democracy has the potential to extend the application of Madison's *republican principle* to the many, appealing to *their cool and deliberate sense of the community* in order to *refine and enlarge the public views by passing them through the medium* [of thoughtful citizen deliberation] *whose wisdom may best discern the true interests of their country, and whose patriotism and love of justice will be least likely to sacrifice it to temporary and partial considerations.*

APPENDIX A

In John Stuart Mill's words, from his *On Liberty*:

> "What the State can usefully do, is to make itself a central depository, and active circulator and diffuser, of the experience resulting from many trials. Its business is to enable each experimentalist to benefit by the experiments of others; instead of tolerating no experiments but its own."

Appendix B

Happiness

In the case of the happiness index, the measurement of both experienced and remembered happiness seems important to us. Daniel Kahneman and Daniel Gilbert make very convincing arguments for the importance of *experienced happiness*. We think that *remembered happiness* might be equally important. Especially in the frame of the organization of communities, which is the main theme of most political essays, including this one.

Income beyond a certain threshold, for example, may not have a much positive effect on our experienced happiness. But this does not necessarily make the drive toward higher incomes so irrational. Perhaps we (unconsciously) do it to enhance our children's start in life.

A similar reasoning may be proposed for childbearing, which we remember as way more pleasant than our actual day-to-day experience of changing diapers. This phenomenon may (unconsciously) encourage us to start families.

Similarly, the euphoria we remember feeling (and expect to feel) when our favorite team wins the national championship may be one of the ingredients of the glue that binds communities together—although our experiencing selves go about their businesses of answering emails and studying for exams the very next day.

Moreover, we can apply this line of thought to the many other phenomena discussed in *Thinking, Fast and Slow* and *Stumbling on Happiness*.

So what may be the common thread that links these phenomena?

In addition to being individual agents, we are part of a larger self which may be seen to

APPENDIX B

include our past, present, and future and, by extension, the lives and stories of our ancestors, descendants, and, again by extension, our communities.

So, in some sense, our self has a nominal unit (Ms. Johnson), a micro-unit (Ms. Johnson's genes, the unit of evolution),* and a macro-unit (Ms. Johnson, her ancestors and descendants, and their stories). And this macro-unit may be seen under an evolutionary light as well.

It is important to measure the *experienced happiness* of people; because, in addition to its intrinsic importance, it may have an impact on people's stress levels and hence on their health, as an example.†

But it seems equally important to us to measure the *remembered happiness* of people; because it may offer an indication of the

---

* So cleverly explained by Richard Dawkins in his *Selfish Gene*

† This is a loose interpretation of Robert Sapolsky's *Why Zebras don't get Ulcers*

prospective well-being of the community, for generations to come.

Let us explain by using a thought experiment (inspired from Kahneman).

An old man (let's call him Mr. Oldman—*sorry*) has led a successful and prosperous life. He passed away peacefully at the age of 92. And he was well appreciated in his community.

Mr. Oldman has founded a loving family. His wife is a charming and smart lady. And his three children all went on to build successful careers and are passionate about their work.

A month after his funeral, we (hypothetically) knock on the neighbors' doors and ask them what they think about Mr. Oldman's life. As expected, most of them answer us that he was a generous and thoughtful man and that he has most certainly led a very happy life.

The following week, it becomes known that Mrs. Oldman had been secretly cheating

APPENDIX B

on her husband for the last 35 years. So we knock again on the neighbors' doors and pose the same question. And this time around, instead of telling us how happy Mr. Oldman was, most of his neighbors tell us that he did not lead such a great life after all because his wife has been cheating on him and hiding it for such a long time.

The first reaction to the neighbors' second comment is that this is completely irrational. The man has already passed away, after all, and he has no way of having felt any less happy about his life. And this line of reasoning makes perfect sense. Mr. Oldman's experienced happiness has not changed at all.

But if we now look at Mr. Oldman's *extended self* (the macro-unit described above) then we might begin to understand why most of us cannot help it but feel a little sad for him. Perhaps we might be (unconsciously) feeling that he was not such a great role model for his children after all; that the values and habits that he transmitted to them are not as flawless as we (or he) once thought. And this may explain the change of opinion.

Mr. Oldman, the nominal unit we usually refer to, is neither more nor less happy. But Mr. Oldman's extended self, which includes his descendants and their stories, may be affected by this revelation. And perhaps this is what makes us feel saddened for him.

So even though higher incomes, children, and football matches do not always enhance our experienced happiness, they most certainly enhance our remembered happiness. Consequently, we may suggest that we have evolved to feel this remembered happiness because income, offspring, and a cohesive society contribute to the future well-being of our community.

In the Declaration of Independence of the United States, Thomas Jefferson writes the following eternal words.

> "We hold these truths to be self-evident, that all men are created equal, that they are endowed by their creator with certain

APPENDIX B

unalienable rights, that among these are life, liberty, and the pursuit of happiness."

This seems beyond a doubt. But *which* happiness should we pursue? And which one counts more to *you*?

Incidentally, this innate predisposition for remembered happiness—which may be explained by our *extended selves*—may also contribute to a favorable environment for the emergence and spread of religion, social norms, and possibly even love.* *But that's another essay!*

---

* At least the kind described by Gibran in his *Prophet*

Appendix C

Morality

We require our executive to be virtuous and act morally. But what exactly is morality?

Kant proposes an elegant answer to this question. He starts by enumerating a number of human qualities. But he quickly complements, or even supersedes, all those qualities by the *good will*.[*]

He goes on to show us the link between the good will and the principle of morality.[†]

---

[*] In his *Fondements de la Métaphysique des Mœurs*, he writes: "les talents de l'esprit ... et les qualités du tempérament, sont sans doute à bien des égards choses bonnes et désirables; mais ces dons de la nature peuvent devenir aussi extrêmement mauvais et funestes si la volonté qui doit en faire usage ... n'est point bonne."

[†] According to Kant: "Est absolument bonne la

A BETTER DEMOCRACY

Kant's categorical imperative is thus formulated: "Act only according to that maxim whereby you can, at the same time, will that it should become a universal law."

In the proposed system, we presume the executive's will to be good, then we invite the people to monitor the executive team and test this assumption on a yearly basis. Which means that the system is built on top of the moral value of reciprocity—the presumption

---

volonté qui ne peut être mauvaise, dont par suite la maxime, quant elle est convertie en loi universelle, ne peut jamais se contredire elle-même."

"Et puisque le caractère qu'a la volonté de valoir comme une loi universelle pour des actions possibles a de l'analogie avec la connexion universelle de l'existence des choses selon des lois universelles, qui est l'élément formel de la nature en général, l'impératif catégorique peut encore s'exprimer ainsi: Agis selon des maximes qui puissent se prendre en même temps elles-mêmes pour objet comme lois universelles de la nature. C'est donc ainsi qu'est constituée la formule d'une volonté absolument bonne."

APPENDIX C

of good faith (the executive team will keep its promise) followed by tit-for-tat (the people withdraw their confidence if it does not). In so doing, it creates a virtuous environment in which cooperation may be fostered. Also, we are not proponents of political immunity. In the proposed democracy, an increase in responsibility leads to an increase in accountability—not to immunity.

Moreover, what Kant and Rawls arrive to through categorical imperatives and what Bentham and Mill arrive to through utilitarianism are, in practical terms, two sides of the same coin: morality favors cooperation, and cooperation—in non-zero-sum systems such as human societies—increases utility.*

Mill seems to flirt with this idea in *Utilitarianism*. In the wonderful introduction to this essay, as he considers the opposition

---

* See Appendix D for more on the emergence and the consequences of cooperation in the proposed system.

between schools of thought concerning the question of the *summum bonum* or the foundation of morality, he writes: "It is true that similar confusion and uncertainty, and in some cases similar discordance, exist respecting the first principles of all sciences, not excepting that which is deemed the most certain of them, mathematics; without much impairing, generally indeed without impairing at all, the trustworthiness of the conclusions of those sciences." And then he seems to consider morals as a science when he suggests that "both [schools of thought] hold equally that morality must be deduced from principles; and the intuitive school affirm as strongly as the inductive, that there is a science of morals."

Mill confirms that both schools arrive to similar moral laws when he writes: "The intuitive, no less than what may be termed the inductive, school of ethics, insists on the necessity of general laws. They both agree that the morality of an individual action is not a question of direct perception, but of

APPENDIX C

the application of a law to an individual case. They recognize also, to a great extent, the same moral laws; but differ as to their evidence, and the source from which they derive their authority."

Our line of thought—that the principles of morality that categorical and utilitarian thinkers arrive at are two sides of the same coin—becomes even clearer when we look at the extended self. In this view, under the veil of ignorance, the chosen principles of justice are those which ensure cooperation in order to maximize the good life of the extended self. Those acts which favor cooperation and hence maximize utility may therefore be considered as moral. And this principle may be adopted as a universal law. In our view, the *ultimate end*, or the purpose of the moral pursuit, lies in biology and not in categorical maxims or in utility for their own sake. But that's another essay.

Furthermore, according to Kant, the good will—which is bound by morality—and the free will are one and the same.*

For Kant, "when we conceive ourselves as free, we transfer ourselves into the world of understanding as members of it and recognize the autonomy of the will with its

---

* According to him: "la liberté, bien qu'elle ne soit pas une propriété de la volonté se conformant à des lois de la nature, n'est pas cependant pour cela en dehors de toute loi; au contraire, elle doit être une causalité agissant selon des lois immuables, mais des lois d'une espèce particulière, car autrement une volonté libre serait un pur rien."

"En quoi donc peut bien consister la liberté de la volonté, sinon dans une autonomie, c'est-à-dire dans la propriété qu'elle a d'être à elle-même sa loi? Or cette proposition: la volonté dans toutes les actions est à elle-même sa loi, n'est qu'une autre formule de ce principe: il ne faut agir que d'après une maxime qui puisse aussi se prendre elle-même pour objet à titre de loi universelle. Mais c'est précisément la formule de l'impératif catégorique et le principe de la moralité; une volonté libre et une volonté soumise à des lois morales sont par conséquent une seule et même chose."

APPENDIX C

consequence, morality."

This conception of free will seems to be consistent with the Rawlsian idea of liberty that is expressed in the first principle of *justice as fairness*. For Rawls, every individual ought to have the most extensive system of basic liberties that is compatible with a similar system of liberty for all others.*

In order to illustrate the link between liberty and morality, and the practical consistency of the utilitarian and categorical views, consider the following excerpt from Mill's *On Liberty*: "The object of this Essay is to assert one very simple principle, as entitled to govern absolutely the dealings of society with the individual in the way of compulsion and control, whether the means used be physical force or in the form of legal penalties, or the moral coercion of public opinion. That principle is, that the sole end for which mankind

---

* See Appendix E for more on the intrinsic justice of the proposed system.

are warranted, individually or collectively, in interfering with the liberty of action of any of their number, is self-protection. That the only purpose for which power can be rightfully exercised over any member of a civilized community, against his will, is to prevent harm to others."

"In the part which merely concerns himself, his independence is, of right, absolute. Over himself, over his own body and mind, the individual is sovereign." This principle is, to our eyes in the least, consistent with the Kantian maxim.

In addition, in line with Mill's thought, thinkers such as Epicurus seem to link morality and justice with the concept of happiness.*
And in their thought, the deepening of

---

* In his *Lettres et Maximes,* he writes: "On ne peut vivre heureux qu'en suivant la prudence, l'honnêteté, la justice; ni pratiquer ces vertus sans être heureux: de sorte que celui qui n'est ni prudent, ni honnête, ni juste ne peut manquer d'être malheureux."

APPENDIX C

knowledge, along with friendship, contribute to happiness.

In the proposed system, we require the executive to demonstrate knowledge by committing to, and achieving measurable outcomes.

The further we think about this topic and the more it becomes evident that there is a strong relation between the concepts of happiness, cooperation, liberty, justice, morality, and knowledge. We may see them as the six facets of one cube. Consequently, the opposition between deontological thinking and teleological thinking seems to concern the thought process more than the practical implications of both schools of philosophy.

Whichever life plan each of us may have, we ought to consider all the facets of the cube if we wish to perfect, advance, progress, or else pursue our personal goals. Someone who wishes to increase his personal experienced happiness, for example, would be well advised to cooperate with others, and therefore act morally. That is because, in non-zero-sum environments in which win-win arrangements are possible, the whole may be greater than the sum of its parts. In other words, this person may end up attaining more personal happiness by cooperating with others instead of pursuing happiness individually.

As another example, someone who enjoys a sense of community and friendship, and therefore who aspires to cooperate, would want to bring something to her relationships with her friends and connections. Assuming healthy, give-and-take associations, this person probably ought to be honest with her peers, she may want to contribute her skills and knowledge, and she may choose to bring fairness and understanding to the group.

Furthermore, all of us intuitively know this from our personal experiences. We all can think of a long list of examples where this simple rule applies: whenever we wish to achieve excellence in our pursuit of personal goals, we would best be advised to consider all six facets of the cube, and avoid neglecting

APPENDIX C

some in favor of others.

In the proposed system, we require the executive to follow the same rule. We ask it to uphold the principles of liberty and justice, to demonstrate knowledge and act morally, in order to foster cooperation and advance happiness, and ultimately the good life of the people.

Appendix D

Cooperation

A beneficial side effect from the shrinking of the community concerns the sense of *experienced responsibility*, which is considered in the text.

In effect, smaller communities may encourage more cooperation among citizens, which leads to more responsible behavior. With the shrinking of our communities, we may expect people to start recognizing each other on the platform as they bump more and more often into one another. And this may induce a change in behavior similar to what one may notice when comparing city and village dwellers.

All of a sudden, individuals who usually barely talk with one another—and who currently find themselves confined within the walls of their favorite party's headquarters, listening to speeches that are sometimes filled with shallow albeit smart-sounding slogans—may discover that *people* lay on the *other side*, and that those people may vote blue on one topic and red on the other, just like themselves.

Let us now consider Robert Axelrod's *Evolution of Cooperation* and frame this topic using *cooperation theory*.

By design, the proposed system seems to favor iterated interactions, both on the level of individuals and of groups. Therefore, it may provide a favorable environment for the emergence of cooperation based on reciprocity.

In the proposed democracy, everyone uses their real identity—*I cannot hide behind a changing pseudonym, alright I get it.*

People who care about similar topics meet one another more frequently on the platform—*here's John Doe again, let me try and be objective and specific in my comment since our*

APPENDIX D

paths keep crossing one another.

Dynamic groups with differing views are bound to interact—*oh well, let's not be so vehement in our language when opposing gay marriage, we all know how the story goes: they will most certainly return the favor when we discuss abortion.*

Commenting histories are public, favoring time-shifted iterated interactions—*oh so my comment may be used against me later on then, ok, good to know.*

And unethical one-off comments are reported and trimmed—*oh so I cannot get away with this hateful comment even though I'm planning to hop on a plane and never look back, gosh this is so unfair.*

In particular, the proposed system seems compatible with the four criteria that promote cooperation, as identified by Axelrod.

First, the *shadow of the future looms large;* indeed, we all remain part of the system—generation after generation—without a specific foreseeable ending or major escape.

A BETTER DEMOCRACY

Second, the *payoffs* encourage cooperation; those who cooperate (constructive conduct, proactivity) may expect medals and knighthood, while those who defect (*ad hominem* attacks, proposals that are contrary to human rights) may expect warnings and penalties.

Third, civic education may be designed to *teach people to care about each other* and to *teach the value of reciprocity;* in particular, the presumption of good faith and the rewards of mutual cooperation—*winning is not a matter of doing better than the other player, but of eliciting cooperation from the other player.*

And fourth, the proposed system may be designed to *improve recognition abilities;* such as the usage of real identities, and the traceability of past interactions.

Furthermore, in Axelrod's model, we do not need to assume that the players are rational, friendly, trusting, or altruistic; we do not even need to assume that they are conscious nor have any foresight… *But we can if we wish to.* Axelrod shows us how cooperation

APPENDIX D

may emerge even among egoists without central authority.

If, under the right conditions, bacteria, algae, fish, primates, and even enemy soldiers can (and indeed do) cooperate, we think that *normal* humans can cooperate as well. And indeed they do.

What's more, even ethics and rituals emerge without many of the above assumptions. So we remain confident that a participative, direct democracy could one day (re)emerge as a stable, robust form of government.

We are not contending that any and all interactions lead to cooperation. The infamous *tragedy of the commons,* and its many real world instances—from deforestation to vandalism—stands as a cautionary counter-example.[*] Instead, our goal is to highlight

---

[*] The tragedy of the commons refers to the depletion of a shared resource by persons acting according to their immediate self-interest. Shepherds sharing a

the importance of ensuring that the right conditions are in place in order for cooperation to occur.

In the end, we are not suggesting that the proposed system, or political life in general, are instances of a strict *prisoner's dilemma* in its fundamental form. However, this direct democracy may be designed as a non-zero-sum environment in which win-win outcomes are achievable.

---

common grazing area, for example, may individually choose to over-utilize it in order to maximize their short-term utility, leading the common to be destroyed to the detriment of all.

Appendix E

Justice

In and of itself, the proposed democracy seems to contribute to the good life of the people—at least in our reading of *A Theory of Justice* by John Rawls.

In fact, justice, and its notions of liberty, equality, and fraternity are prerequisites for the good life. In our view, the latter cannot be conceived except in the light of the principles of liberty and justice. And in his inspiring work, Rawls proposes two principles of justice:

1. Each person is to have an equal right to the most extensive total system of equal basic liberties compatible with a similar system of liberty for all.
2. Social and economic inequalities are

to be arranged so that they are both:

a To the greatest benefit of the least advantaged, consistent with the just savings principle, and

b Attached to offices and positions open to all under conditions of fair equality of opportunity.

On the first principle, he proposes that: "The basic liberties of citizens are, roughly speaking, political liberty (the right to vote and to be eligible for public office) together with freedom of speech and assembly; liberty of conscience and freedom of thought; freedom of the person along with the right to hold (personal) property; and freedom from arbitrary arrest and seizure as defined by the concept of the rule of law."

In his *On Liberty*, Mill expresses a similar view: "This, then, is the appropriate region of human liberty. It comprises, first, the inward domain of consciousness; demanding liberty

APPENDIX E

of conscience, in the most comprehensive sense; liberty of thought and feeling; absolute freedom of opinion and sentiment on all subjects, practical or speculative, scientific, moral, or theological. The liberty of expressing and publishing opinions may seem to fall under a different principle, since it belongs to that part of the conduct of an individual which concerns other people; but, being almost of as much importance as the liberty of thought itself, and resting in great part on the same reasons, is practically inseparable from it. Secondly, the principle requires liberty of tastes and pursuits; of framing the plan of our life to suit our own character; of doing as we like, subject to such consequences as may follow: without impediment from our fellow creatures, so long as what we do does not harm them, even though they should think our conduct foolish, perverse, or wrong. Thirdly, from this liberty of each individual, follows the liberty, within the same limits, of combination among individuals; freedom to unite, for any purpose not involving harm to others: the persons combining being supposed to be of full age, and not forced or deceived."

On the second principle, Rawls proposes that: "the higher expectations of those better situated are just if and only if they work as part of a scheme which improves the expectations of the least advantaged members of society." And that "positions of authority and offices of command must be accessible to all."

It seems to us that the proposed democracy is, by construction, consistent with the Rawlsian theory.

Liberty. In fact, concerning the first principle, the institutions we are suggesting seem to enhance the basic liberties of all citizens—political liberty and freedom of speech and assembly, in particular.

It seems evident to us that the power of lawmaking—the ability to propose, debate and vote on law—and the novel involvement in the executive process are firm steps in the

APPENDIX E

direction of more *extensive equal basic liberties compatible with similar liberties for all.*

Equality. In addition, thanks to the lowered barrier to entry, the suggested institutions seem to be compatible with the second principle as well. The proposed democracy seems to promote fair equality of opportunity—because citizens have a fairer chance to participate in public life and hold political responsibilities and offices.

Presumably, not everyone can make an equal impact on the political process—because this depends on each individual's talents; such as her intelligence, eloquence, perseverance, and the like. But all those who have similar political abilities and skills would have more similar chances to realize them in our direct democracy.

Fraternity. Furthermore, a strong incentive for *those who have been favored by nature* is built into the proposed system so that they *may gain from their good fortune only in terms that improve the situation of those who have lost out.* Thanks to the participation of all in the political process, *the naturally advantaged are not to gain merely because they are more gifted, but for using their endowments in ways that help the less fortunate.* That is because all citizens, gifted or less gifted, can make their voices directly heard, and thereby influence the public agenda.

In a sense, since it seems to increase liberty, equality, and fraternity, the proposed system renders our society more just. And a just society allows the good life of the people.

Therefore, in addition to the potential benefits from direct participation in lawmaking and the control of the executive (i.e. the utility, or prospect, of the outcome), the proposed democracy seems to contribute intrinsically to the good life of the people, through the justice of its institutions.

APPENDIX E

By the way, there may be a link between *justice* and the concept of the *extended self* that we mentioned earlier. That is because, under the Rawlsian veil of ignorance, we decide upon principles of justice without a prior knowledge of our social status or talent. In fact, our social status and talent affect our initial chances in life. However, under the theory of justice, they cannot be justified by an appeal to the notion of merit. We do not have any merit in being born in a wealthy family, for example.

Which is undeniable.

Except when we look at the individual within his macro-unit—the extended self that comprises a person's ancestors and descendants. Then we may arrive at the paradox that there is perhaps some merit to be acknowledged when a father works hard to ensure a good start in life for his daughter.

But that's another essay as well!

Notes

You should not need to read the following notes unless you feel a little more interested (or skeptical) about certain ideas.

If you are of the curious type, however, we do recommend the appendices. Appendix A is a deeper dive into the circumstances and the meaning of deliberation. Appendix B is an attempt to go a little further into the concept of happiness, and into the meaning of remembered happiness, in particular. Appendix C is a peak into the concept, and ramifications, of morality. Appendix D is a brief look at cooperation theory—how does cooperation emerge and when. And Appendix E is a nod to the theory of justice, why we think that the proposed democracy is fundamentally just and what this means for the good life.

As a side note, we are referring to this work as an *essay* with the French etymology in mind: *essai* as in trial or attempt. So please feel free to send your thoughts, feedback, and critique to better.democracy.essay@gmail.com.

In the end, the elements that are discussed here are by no means definite. We see them as a handful of simple ideas, a few humble steps on the long path of building our republic.

In the words of John Stuart Mill:

> "Truth gains more even by the errors of one who, with due study and preparation, thinks for himself, than by the true opinions of those who only hold them because they do not suffer themselves to think."

Notes to the Introduction

1 This statement is applicable to so-called developed countries, which we are taking as a starting point to (hopefully) improve upon.
2 We are often fooled by a narrative fallacy,

a sense of causality (event A lead to event B), when looking at past historical events. See *Thinking, Fast and Slow* by Daniel Kahneman for a great read on this topic (and many more).

3   Centers of the Babylonian, Macedonian, Inca, and Mongol Empires

4   What is commonly referred to as modern democracies: the several variants of representative democracies that one may find in northern America or western Europe, for example

5   We cannot but be tempted by John Rawls' definition of good, in his *Theory of Justice*, when he writes: "something's being good is its having the properties that it is rational to want in things of its kind."

In this essay, we are specifying the *good* (the good life, which is the end to be achieved), and interpreting the *right* as a way to arrive at it (a political system that enables the good life of citizens). This may be akin to a perfectionist approach.

However, since the concept of good life

applies to society and is governed by the notion of justice—along with liberty and equality—we do not see the risk of oppression or exploitation arising.

6   From *Government in the Future*, by Noam Chomsky who cites Wilhelm Von Humboldt's *Limits of State Action*: "To inquire and create—these are the centers around which all human pursuits more or less directly revolve."

In a complementary—higher order—view, the good life must emancipate us to fulfill our "desire to express most fully what we are or can be, namely free and equal rational beings with a liberty to choose." That is if we were to cite freely from Rawls's Kantian interpretation of justice as fairness.

And, if we were to take this one step further, then we may consider that when these conditions are not fulfilled, we ought to turn to indignation and action—at least according to one interpretation of Stéphane Hessel. In his *Indignez Vous*, Hessel considers indifference as the worst of attitudes toward the unbearable. "En vous comportant ainsi, vous perdez l'une des composantes essentielles qui fait l'humain. Une des composantes indispensables: la faculté d'indignation et l'engagement qui en est la conséquence."

In allowing for the pursuit of the good life, the proposed democracy offers concrete ways for citizens to channel such emotions constructively for the benefit of the broader community, as we will see further below.

7 In *The Politics*, Aristotle ends his sentence with "... by men acting together."
8 By a factor of several hundred when we compare ancient city-states to modern industrial nations
9 Right of women to vote and the abolition of slavery, in particular
10 Representative democracies, such as our current governments, are systems in which, instead of deliberating directly with one another, we delegate this responsibility to representatives (members of parliament or congressmen) who do it on our behalf.
11 Electoral programs are also known as *party*

platforms in some countries

12 See *The Righteous Mind* by Jonathan Haidt on the relation between people's moral values and their political leaning—liberals, for example, tend to value care and fairness more than loyalty, authority and purity.

See also Steven Pinker's *The Blank Slate* on the link between liberal and conservative attitudes and the temperaments of people—conservatives, for example, tend to be more authoritarian, conscientious, traditional, and rule bound.

13 As in Nassim Taleb's Epistemocracy, described in his *Black Swan*

Notes to the Legislative Element

1 This system would also repeal the typical role of senator from most western democracies.
2 In the fields of telecommunication and networking, and decision-making and psychology, in particular

3 "One does not need to be a good writer to vote on the book of the year, he only needs to be a good reader," one may think when reading the preceding statement.

So even though the citizens may not be required, in our modern democracies, to master the process of lawmaking, they are assumed to understand the impact of laws.

"Candidate X is promising to oppose raising taxes, I understand the impacts and agree/disagree, and so I vote for/against him," a voter may think. So our current democracies assume, *a minima,* a citizen understanding of the impacts of lawmaking.

At this point, the assumption of this know-how suffices for our argument.

4 For example in health, economics, or agriculture, to name a few

5 Madam Martin, 70 years old, living in Marseille in a small apartment with an old dog, may perhaps not wish (because of lack of know-how, for example) to debate nor vote on a bill pertaining to nuclear energy. (Physicists, on the other hand, may feel more

comfortable debating this topic.)

But Madam Martin will probably take part in the conversations around retirement and social security. Under the current system, she delegates her vote on all of the issues to a single member of parliament who might disagree with her on social security and not know any better about nuclear energy.

6   Because those individuals are necessarily part of the larger population; and also because the proposed system contains a strong deliberative element, which allows this collective knowledge to emerge—a mechanic that stands in contrast to top of the head opinions on policy.

7   Daniel Pink, *Drive*

8   Pink gives Wikipedia as an example of a project built by volunteering individuals, who were not paid, and ended up building the world's largest encyclopedia. Mozilla Firefox, the free open-source web browser, is another such example.

9   See *How Australians Use Their Time* by the Australian Bureau of Statistics, for example,

or *How is the time of women and men distributed in Europe* by Christel Aliaga

10 Which is less than 5 minutes per day, or half an hour per week and per person. This is of course an average: some will spend more, others less.

We can imagine that some individuals would dedicate more time to this process (perhaps some of the current politicians, a few academics, some thinkers, or a number of activists), thereby helping the larger society connect the dots among the arguments and public choices being made.

And given the current levels of participation, deliberation, and equality, this may be a significant step forward.

11 Noise pollution for Jane, child care for John, and speed limits for Lisa

12 Which seems generous, judging by the all too common pictures of half empty hemicycles

13 By no means definite

14 Responsible and lasting power, that is. Giving someone power without knowledge feels like a recipe for disaster. That is because, with

time, they will invariably do wrong. Or so we shall argue.

15 From one's computer at home, using a Google-style search engine, for example

16 So the law takes a metaphorical step toward the people (simplification), and the people take a step toward the law (training).

17 Conseil d'État, *Sécurité juridique et complexité du droit*

18 Such as codes pertaining to solidarity, community, education, health, the environment, economy and international relations, for example

19 To avoid ending up with two laws instead of one

20 "Il ne faut point faire par les lois ce qu'on peut faire par les mœurs." Montesquieu, *Pensées Diverses*

21 Philip Howard, *Life Without Lawyers*

22 Simplification of law should not be taken to the other extreme.

We think that a golden mean exists in which law is not overly complicated and, in the same time, justice can still be served. That is, the rule of law must still apply—justice as regularity and the precept that similar cases be treated similarly, in particular.

23 This section is generally based on Daniel Martin's thoughtful research and analysis, which he explains (much better) on danielmartin.eu.

24 This famous citation, *nul n'est censé ignorer la loi*, which is attributed to Aristotle, has a longer form that seems to support the idea of simplification and training: *nobody is supposed to be ignorant of the law, especially when it is easy to know.*

25 During those sessions, which could take place at nearby courthouses, people would discuss with judges and lawyers from their community.

26 About 20 miles per hour. The current speed limit within cities in a country like France is 50 km/h (or about 30 miles per hour).

27 This essay is not advocating any particular policy.
Reducing the speed limit is an arbitrary example to illustrate the legislative process.

If you do not agree with Lisa, you can always vote against her proposal as we will see further below!

28 Lisa has to use her real identity in order to login to this political platform. This is, after all, a virtual replication of a participative democracy.

Identified login has the added benefit of dramatically reducing spam and hate comments and furthering cooperation—as we will see further below.

29 In such a system, people will sponsor a proposal primarily for its content, but also because Lisa behaves as a team player who welcomes the suggestions and ideas of others in order to complement and improve her own ideas.

30 About 50,000 endorsements in a country the size of France

31 An amendment can, as in this case, change the function of the law (e.g. reduced speed from 50 to 30 km/h) or change its form (e.g. simplify the wording of a law, group related laws into one).

32 We may imagine that, through the proposal of bills, the executive may give guidance and influence the public debate.

In all cases, the key philosophical change is that this process becomes open to all—and this, in itself, is a firm step toward a better democracy.

33 In the cases where the proposal is anti-constitutional (e.g. not in conformity with human rights), citizens may report it as such and a community of judges will promptly examine the contention and suppress the proposal, giving its author a warning along the way.

34 An algorithm allows citizens to sort the arguments (from their group and from the larger community) by level of engagement and agreeability so that the most insightful and poignant arguments become easily accessible.

35 Or 500,000 people in a country the size of France

36 We are focusing on Lisa for clarity. It may be that several citizens propose a bill together, nurture it, and follow up on it all the way to

the voting stage.

Also for the sake of clarity, we are focusing on one level of government (national or state level). But similar concepts may apply to local government, as well.

37 From his *Areopagitica*, cited by Kenneth Arrow in his *Social Choice and Individual Values*

38 We may expect law projects in the final stages to be mentioned by news outlets and discussed widely within the society.

39 There is no need for a participation quorum in a direct democracy because they are contradictory with the mandate principle as shown by Jos Verhulst and Arjen Nijeboer in their Direct Democracy.

However, to make changes to the constitution, half of all eligible citizens must approve the amendment (or 25 million people in a country the size of France), regardless of the number of voters. We see the constitution as a set of concise, fundamental principles—namely the constitutional powers of government and the basic rights of citizens.

40 When a citizen casts her vote, she is given a randomly generated unique identifier (e.g. AABJ-54092748) for the ballot. The identifier is not publicly linked to the voter's identity and so the ballot remains secret. However, the identifier allows any citizen to compare her vote with the published record—thereby collectively controlling the vote. David Bismark proposed this idea. He describes it further (and better) on evoting.bismark.se.

41 Perhaps around 10 projects of law being advertised and another 10 under vote (this is only a guess, to help illustrate the matter)

42 The sub-title of this essay—Sixty-five million people at the Palais Bourbon—is a nod to the idea that we all have a Lisa within us. We too can become legislators (equality). In fact, sixty-five million is the population of France (participation), and the Palais Bourbon is the seat of the French National Assembly (deliberation).

43 Who would not appreciate to be knighted for their contributions to society!?

44 An added benefit of the medals is their game

mechanics aspect—we may expect this to drive engagement in the process. Such symbols and titles, with the rituals that are associated to them, may become a part of the larger culture.

Another benefit from medals is their contribution to the emergence of cooperation, as will be discussed further below.

45 John Locke, in his *Two Treatises of Government*, looks at human nature to arrive at political principles: "To understand political power right, and derive it from its original, we must consider what state all men are naturally in, and that is, a state of perfect freedom to order their actions and dispose of their possessions and persons, as they think fit, within the bounds of the law of nature, without asking leave, or depending upon the will of any other man."

"A state also of equality, wherein all the power and jurisdiction is reciprocal, no one having more than an other; there being nothing more evident, than that creatures of the same species and rank, promiscuously born to all the same advantages of nature, and the use of the same faculties, should also be equal one amongst another without subordination or subjection."

46 For example, in Adam Smith's *Wealth of Nations*, when the economic system is left alone, it tends to take care of itself. "As every individual endeavours to employ his capital so that its produce may be of the greatest value, he necessarily labours to render the revenue of the society as great as he can. He generally, indeed, neither intends to promote the public interest, nor knows how much he is promoting it. And he is in this, as in many other cases, led by an invisible hand to promote an end which was no part of his intention." Paraphrased.

Similarly in our proposal, every citizen promotes the public interest as he advocates the topics that are closest to his heart.

In fact, the proposed system, if well organized and adapted, may play a role similar to that of the price system in a free market as described by Friedrich Hayek in his *The Use of Knowledge in Society* when he writes: "a little reflection will show that there is beyond question a body of very important but unorganized knowledge which cannot possibly be called scientific in the sense of knowledge of general rules: the knowledge of the particular circumstances of time and place. It is with respect to this that practically every individual has some advantage over all others in that he possesses unique information of which beneficial use might be made, but of which use can be made only if the decisions depending on it are left to him or are made with his active cooperation."

"Fundamentally, in a system where the knowledge of the relevant facts is dispersed among many people, prices can act to coordinate the separate actions of different people in the same way as subjective values help the planner to coordinate the parts of his plan."

"We must look at the price system as such a mechanism for communicating information if we want to understand its real function."

In a similar manner, important *political*

knowledge of the particular circumstances of time and place is dispersed among most citizens. Furthermore, their voices—ideas, proposals, arguments, insights, research, and experience—are communicated through the proposed system and, without a central planner having to propose some legislative *ordre du jour,* without a party bureau that sets legislative priorities or committees that author predefined bills, those voices that deserve to, end up becoming law.

Hayek hits the nail on the head when he continues: "The problem is precisely how to extend the span of our utilization of resources beyond the span of control of any one mind; and, therefore, how to dispense with the need of conscious control and how to provide inducements which will make the individuals do the desirable things without anyone having to tell them what to do."

"The problem with which we meet here is by no means peculiar to economics but arises in connection with nearly all truly social phenomena, with language and most of our cultural inheritance, and constitutes really the central theoretical problem of all social science."

"The price system is just one of those formations which man has learned to use (though he is very far from having learned to make the best use of it) after having stumbled upon it without understanding it."

Notes to the Executive Element

1 The fulfillment of objectives ought to be measurable (99% literacy...), and have a deadline (...within 5 years).
2 If they have proposed bills which went on to become law, for example. So our friend Lisa may be part of one such group.
3 Or 2.5 million people in a country about the size of France.

Citizens may endorse more than one program each, thereby contributing to a more nuanced political environment (instead of

Notes to page 33

clear-cut right-or-wrong judgments).

Also, the thresholds that are given throughout the text are for illustrative purposes. We may very well imagine that they would be adapted to achieve the best outcomes. For example, if 5% proves too high a threshold and not enough programs are endorsed, it may be lowered—and vice versa.

4 These deliberations take place within the previously described deliberative groups of 500+ randomly selected citizens. They are akin to the Athenian mayoral selection described in James Fishkin's *When the People Speak*.

5 We are not assuming voters to be economically rational (like the so-called *homo economicus*), just human.

See Dan Ariely's *Predictably Irrational* for fun, yet insightful examples of the many ways we are *just* human.

And in *Games People Play*, while discussing the basic difference between mathematical and transactional game analysis, Eric Berne writes: "Mathematical game analysis postulates players who are completely rational.

Transactional game analysis deals with games which are un-rational, or even irrational, and hence more real."

6   Frank Knight's statement, in his *Economic Theory and Nationalism* is interesting in this regard: "The principle of majority rule must be taken ethically as a means of ascertaining a real 'general will,' not as a mechanism by which one set of interests is made subservient to another set. Political discussion must be assumed to represent a quest for an objectively ideal or 'best' policy, not a contest between interests." (Cited by Kenneth Arrow in his *Social Choice and Individual Values*)

7   It seems that Alice—our favorite fabricated voter—either does not have much confidence in Chris and his team, or does not approve of their proposals.

8   One tactical voting method is the so-called *useful vote* in countries with two dominant parties. In such countries, many voters choose the least of two evils between the two main candidates when their preferred candidate has little chance of winning. Basically,

according to this terminology, if you choose a third candidate, your vote is not useful—it is useless.

According to Kenneth Arrow, in his *Social Choice and Individual Values*: "in an electoral system based on plurality voting, it is notorious that an individual who really favors a minor party candidate will frequently vote for the less undesirable of the major party candidates rather than 'throw away his vote.'" Similar shortcomings have been present, and decried, since the nineteenth century. In his *Considerations on Representative Government*, Mill offers the following account: "The electors who are on a different side in party politics from the local majority, are unrepresented. Of those who are on the same side, a large proportion are misrepresented; having been obliged to accept the man who had the greatest number of supporters in their political party, though his opinions may differ from theirs on every other point. The state of things is, in some respects, even worse than if the minority were not allowed to vote at all; for then, at least the majority might have a member who would represent their own best mind: while now, the necessity of not dividing the party, for fear of letting in its opponents, induces all to vote either for the first person who presents himself wearing their colours, or for the one brought forward by their local leaders; and these, if we pay them the compliment, which they very seldom deserve, of supposing their choice to be unbiased by their personal interests, are compelled, that they may be sure of mustering their whole strength, to bring forward a candidate whom none of the party will strongly object to—that is, a man without any distinctive peculiarity, any known opinions except the shibboleth of the party."

9   In effect, the more popular first-past-the-post system (in which voters select only one candidate) tends to propel two candidates (or two coalitions) forward, thereby diluting their proposals to the lowest common denominator, which usually is a binary moral stand (liberal or conservative) instead of the fuller

spectrum of available policy alternatives.

In his *On Liberty*, John Stuart Mill tells us: "Unless opinions favourable to democracy and to aristocracy, to property and to equality, to co-operation and to competition, to luxury and to abstinence, to sociality and individuality, to liberty and discipline, and all the other standing antagonisms of practical life, are expressed with equal freedom, and enforced and defended with equal talent and energy, there is no chance of both elements obtaining their due; one scale is sure to go up, and the other down. Truth, in the great practical concerns of life, is so much a question of the reconciling and combining of opposites."

"When there are persons to be found, who form an exception to the apparent unanimity of the world on any subject, even if the world is in the right, it is always probable that dissentients have something worth hearing to say for themselves, and that truth would lose something by their silence."

10 From this point forward, we will make the

following two associations: the people vote to express their confidence in the executive team (confidence/team) and their approval of the executive program (approval/program).

11 A role which is typically held by the council of ministers (in countries such as France, Italy or the Netherlands) or the cabinet (in the United States or the United Kingdom)

12 Rousseau describes the *pacte social*, in his *Du Contrat Social* as a state in which "chacun de nous met en commun sa personne et toute sa puissance sous la suprême direction de la volonté générale, et nous recevons en corps chaque membre comme partie indivisible du tout. A l'instant, au lieu de la personne particulière de chaque contractant, cet acte d'association produit un corps moral et collectif composé d'autant de membres que l'assemblée a de voix."

13 Two successive disapprovals of programs lead to reelections.

Programs are designed to cover a mandate of five years. So the nominal case is one where the Council of Ministers is performing well and delivering satisfactory results year after year, in which case confidence and approval are granted happily by the people who can now measure the progress and compare it to the program instead of having to compare it to changing arguments and rhetoric.

In the cases where the Council of Ministers appears to the people to be unworthy of confidence or, its members being well appreciated, its program becomes irrelevant to a changing context, then change is called for by the vote.

14 Still measurable and timely
15 On average as with the legislative process, since some people will contribute more, and others less.

In *On Liberty*, Mill writes: "for what more or better can be said of any condition of human affairs, than that it brings human beings themselves nearer to the best thing they can be? Or what worse can be said of any obstruction to good, than that it prevents this?"

"There is always need of persons not only to discover new truths, and point out when what were once truths are true no longer, but also to commence new practices, and set the example of more enlightened conduct, and better taste and sense in human life."

"It is true that this benefit is not capable of being rendered by everybody alike: there are but few persons, in comparison with the whole mankind, whose experiments, if adopted by others, would be likely to be any improvement on established practice. But these few are the salt of the earth; without them, human life would become a stagnant pool."

"Persons of genius, it is true, are, and are always likely to be, a small minority; but in order to have them, it is necessary to preserve the soil in which they grow. Genius can only breathe freely in an *atmosphere* of freedom."

"Meanwhile, recollecting that nothing was ever yet done which some one was not the first to do, and that all good things which exist are the fruits of originality, let [us] be modest enough to believe that there is something still left for it to accomplish, and assure [ourselves] that [we] are more in need of originality, the less [we] are conscious of the want."

"All he [the person of genius] can claim is, freedom to point out the way. The power of compelling others into it, is not only inconsistent with the freedom and development of all the rest, but corrupting to the strong man himself."

"It is in these circumstances most especially, that exceptional individuals, instead of being deterred, should be encouraged in acting differently from the mass."

"Eccentricity has alway abounded when and where strength of character has abounded; and the amount of eccentricity in a society has generally been proportional to the amount of genius, mental vigour, and moral courage which it contained. That so few now dare to be eccentric, marks the chief danger of the time."

In Mill's view, it is diversity that makes the difference between human progressiveness and stationary societies. He cites Von

Humboldt when he writes that 'the end of man, or that which is prescribed by the eternal or immutable dictates of reason, and not suggested by vague and transient desires, is the highest and most harmonious development of his powers to a complete and consistent whole'; that, therefore, the object 'towards which every human being must ceaselessly direct his efforts, and on which especially those who design to influence their fellow men must ever keep their eyes, is the individuality of power and development'; that for this there are two requisites, 'freedom, and variety of situations'; and that from the union of these arise 'individual vigour and manifold diversity', which combine themselves in 'originality'.

16 These continuous assessments and corrections seem, in effect, to have an interesting side-benefit. Daniel Gilbert proposes in his *Stumbling on Happiness*, that we (humans) sometimes have an illusion of foresight, and "we assume that what we feel as we imagine the future is what we'll feel when we get

there, but in fact, what we feel as we imagine the future is often a response to what's happening in the present."

So we might just as well allow ourselves the opportunity to reassess and change our minds, as is suggested in the proposed system.

17 It is in line with the spirit of John Locke's following statement from his *Two Treatises of Government*: "Whensoever the legislative shall transgress this fundamental rule of society; and either by ambition, fear, folly or corruption, endeavour to grasp themselves, or put into the hands of any other, an absolute power over the lives, liberties, and estates of the people; by this breach of trust they forfeit the power the people had put into their hands for quite contrary ends, and it devolves to the people, who have a right to resume their original liberty, and, by the establishment of a new legislative, (such as they shall think fit) provide for their own safety and security, which is the end for which they are in society.

What I have said here, concerning the legislative in general, holds true also concerning the supreme executor, who having a double trust put in him, both to have a part in the legislative, and the supreme execution of the law, acts against both, when he goes about to set up his own arbitrary will as the law of the society."

It is also in line with Karl Popper's suggestion, in his *Open Society and its Enemies* of "governments of which we can get rid without bloodshed—for example, by way of general elections; that is to say, the social institutions provide means by which the rulers may be dismissed by the ruled, and the social traditions ensure that these institutions will not easily be destroyed by those who are in power."

And in his *Theory of Justice*, John Rawls tells us that, in a just constitution, "the authority to determine basic social policies resides in a representative body selected for limited terms by and ultimately *accountable to* the electorate." Emphasis is ours.

18 At least until (if ever) we arrive at a reliable *physics of society*, of the type that one senses when reading Philip Ball's *Critical Mass*. Meanwhile, empiricism—which is based on experience and evidence—seems like a more appropriate attitude.
19 Including by the body of citizens in its choice of the government and its policy
20 Any number of objectives, however measurable or timely, can never fully represent the complexity of public life. A system such as the one presented here seems to deal well with the unexpected.

In his *Considerations on Representative Government*, Mill gives us an idea of the complexity of ensuring a virtuous and intelligent performance of all the duties of government when he writes: "Good laws would be established and enforced, bad laws would be reformed; the best men would be placed in all situations of trust; justice would be as well administered, the public burthens would be as light and as judiciously imposed, every branch of administration would be as purely and as intelligently conducted, as the circumstances of the country and its degree of intellectual and moral cultivation would admit."

21 In his *Considerations on Representative Government*, Mill writes: "There is a radical distinction between controlling the business of government, and actually doing it. The same person or body may be able to control everything; and in many cases its control over everything will be more perfect, the less it personally attempts to do. The commander of an army could not direct its movements effectually if he himself fought in the ranks, or led an assault. It is the same with bodies of men. Some things cannot be done except by bodies; other things cannot be well done by them. It is one question, therefore, what a popular assembly should control, another what it should itself do. It should, as we have already seen, control all the operations of government. But in order to determine through what channel this general control may most expediently be exercised, and what

portion of the business of government the representative body should hold in its own hands, it is necessary to consider what kind of business a numerous body is competent to perform properly. That alone which it can do well, it ought to take personally upon itself. With regard to the rest, its proper province is not to do it, but to take means for having it well done by others."

And then, describing the employment of a representative assembly, he adds: "A place where every interest and shade of opinion in the country can have its cause even passionately pleaded, in the face of the government and of all other interests and opinions, can compel them to listen, and either comply, or state clearly why they do not, is in itself, if it answered no other purpose, one of the most important political institutions that can exist anywhere, and one of the foremost benefits of free government."

22 Such an engagement is of paramount importance even in our current systems, especially when the legislative and executive powers

are in the hands of the same party—the risk of a reduced citizen engagement is all too obvious: one and the same party decides the rules (lawmaking) and carries out policy (execution).

23 Using checks and balances and the separation of powers, for example
24 In cases of conflict of interest, in particular
25 Such as limited political advertisement and a rigorous political coverage in the media. Why not define criteria (citation of sources and affiliations, picture and video editing requirements…) for a broadcast program or article to earn a *political stamp* of quality, for example?

The honesty and justice of our political system are also directly affected by campaign spending: Limited and equal campaign budgets improve the clarity of political choice and ensure a better equality of opportunity.

A similar reasoning applies to spending and advertisement on legislative topics.

In his *Considerations on Representative Government,* John Stuart Mill argues that: "So long as the elected member, in any shape or manner, pays for his seat, all endeavours will fail to make the business of election anything but a selfish bargain on all sides. So long as the candidate himself, and the customs of the world, seem to regard the function of a member of Parliament less as a duty to be discharged, than a personal favour to be solicited, no effort will avail to implant in an ordinary voter the feeling that the election of a member of Parliament is also a matter of duty, and that he is not at liberty to bestow his vote on any other consideration than that of personal fitness."

26 Transparency can be seen in the light of relative power: more privacy for individuals and less secrecy for governments (e.g. governmental documents cannot remain indefinitely confidential).

As such, we are proponents of a wider access to governmental data, at least to the extent of giving the people access to the data that is currently accessible by members of parliament.

27 Aristotle, *The Politics*

28 Plato, *The Republic*

Even Sun Tzu's commander, described in his *Art of War*, among other virtues, has to have wisdom, integrity, compassion, and courage.

29 (The illustrations on the front and back covers, mixing thinkers with statesmen, are a nod to this idea.) In previous versions, the front cover depicted an Einstein crossing the Alps while on the back cover Washington was shown listening carefully as Aristotle and Plato conversed.

30 For example, by proposing 10 bills or more which end up becoming law, without having been a declared candidate for elections in the past

31 And each president serves up to two years. The council members are not all replaced at once. And this ensures continuity in the council's composition.

Of course, the number of presidents composing the council, five in this case, is arbitrary. It is meant to illustrate the idea.

32 The head of state is a different role from that of prime minister.

A president of the republic typically holds this role (or a Monarch in constitutional monarchies). In Switzerland, a seven-member council fulfills this function.

We propose to separate this role from that of prime minister to allow for more separation of powers. In countries with a presidential system, such as the United States, one individual holds both roles (head of state and head of government). In other countries, such as Germany and Italy, those two roles are held by two people—the president and the chancellor, in the case of Germany; the president and the prime minister in the case of Italy.

33 An important, albeit romantic concept.

Charles De Gaulle for example, a notorious head of state, had this to write about France in his *Mémoires de Guerre*: "Toute ma vie, je me suis fait une certaine idée de la France… Le sentiment me l'inspire aussi bien que la raison.

Ce qu'il y a, en moi, d'affectif imagine naturellement la France, telle la princesse des contes ou la madone aux fresques des murs, comme vouée à une destinée éminente et exceptionnelle. Que notre pays, tel qu'il est, parmi les autres, tels qu'ils sont, doit, sous peine de danger mortel, viser haut et se tenir droit.

Bref, à mon sens, la France ne peut être la France sans la grandeur."

George Washington, another remarkable head of state, had the following to say in his *First Inaugural Speech*: "I was summoned by my Country, whose voice I can never hear but with veneration and love, from a retreat which I had chosen with the fondest predilection."

34 In his *Politics*, Aristotle tells us that: "The mixture of lot and suffrage, and the appointment to some deliberative functions in the one way, and to other deliberative functions in the other, is consonant to the nature of what we call a republic."

35 "Le suffrage par le sort est de la nature de la démocratie; le suffrage par choix est de celle de l'aristocratie.

Le sort est une façon d'élire qui n'afflige personne, il laisse à chaque citoyen une espérance raisonnable." *Esprit des Lois*, Montesquieu

Notes to the Conclusion

1 Inspired from a statement by the Parti de Gauche in France: "La République est toujours davantage un projet à réaliser qu'un simple ensemble d'institutions."
2 At least to the general discussion surrounding this project
3 That being said, a political transition of this kind must probably be gradual and spread in time. In the case of the proposed democracy, for example, the educational curriculum ought to be adapted and enough citizens trained. And prior to the suppression of parliament, people ought to be invited to vote on more and more laws—perhaps moderated by their representatives at first, another possibility would be for votes to be held following

deliberative polls. A gradual increase in the number of referendums may also be helpful... In any case, a clear step-by-step implementation (which needs not be entirely conscious) of such a system is out of the scope of this first work.

4 Said metaphorically, we do not really care whether human beings are Voltaire's *Candide* or Machiavelli's *Prince*.

5 Robert Axelrod's *The Evolution of Cooperation* is a must read on the topic of the emergence of viable, stable, and robust cooperation between individuals who are pursuing their own interests; and we will get back to his edifying work further below.

6 The sense of responsibility that is felt by an individual

7 It is representatives who denied women the right to vote, then went on to grant it (as late as 1944 in the case of France). Other representatives decided that slavery was right, before correcting their stance and abolishing it (in 1865, after a bloody civil war, in the case of the United States). And contemporary

examples of bad law abound.

8 Let us be clear here. We are neither advocating a patriarchal society, nor a return to the unethical system of slavery. And it is not with cynicism that we look at this state of affairs, but with optimism. We are optimistic about the continuous improvement of our societies.

9 Today women have the right to vote. Slavery has been abolished. And hopefully, a hundred years from today we will look back and see all the progress that we have accomplished as a society since the year 2010.

Actually, article 26 of the French constitution explicitly protects the opinions and positions of members of parliament (and thankfully so): "Aucun membre du Parlement ne peut être poursuivi, recherché arrêté, détenu ou jugé à l'occasion des opinions ou votes émis par lui dans l'exercice de ses fonctions."

Far from a falling, resilience and the correction of errors are some of the most important human virtues. In John Stuart Mill's words: "Why is it, then, that there is on the whole a preponderance among mankind of rational opinions and rational conduct? If there really is this preponderance—which there must be unless human affairs are, and have always been, in an almost desperate state—it is owing to a quality of the human mind, the source of everything respectable in man either as an intellectual or as a moral being, namely, that his errors are corrigible. He is capable of rectifying his mistakes, by discussion and experience."

"Wrong opinions and practices gradually yield to fact and argument."

10 We may take the metaphor of the people moving from childhood to adulthood to illustrate the increased empowerment and accountability of citizens.

11 By the way, the taxes thought experiment could very well have been constructed with the opposite outcome. The mass of the people may end up increasing taxes (perhaps on high income individuals). We simply cannot tell in advance. It can be one extreme or the other, one followed by the other, or anything in between. But it does not matter much.

Notes to page 54

In all cases, the system learns from experience, corrects, and stabilizes. It may even go into successive stable states in a changing environment.

12 In his *A Constitution for Knaves Crowds out Civic Virtues*, Bruno Frey surveyed Swiss cantons looking for a connection between the system of democracy and the citizens' attitude to taxes. He found that the amount of undeclared revenue in cantons where people have extensive rights of participation in decision-making is much lower than in cantons with less direct democracy.

In other words, people seem to cheat less and pay more taxes under direct democracy.

In another comparative study of Swiss cantons by Lars Feld and Marcel Savioz, reported in their *Direct Democracy Matters for Economic Performance*, the authors found that economic performance increases with the level of direct democracy.

And in yet another study by Lars Feld, Gebhard Kirchgässner, and Marcel Savioz, discussed in their *Die Direkte Demokratie*, the authors found that, other things being equal, direct democracy contributes to reducing (not to increasing) public debt—through the people's involvement in the decisions on public expenditure.

In all those cases, the people seem to act more (not less) responsibly as the level of direct democracy increases.

Jos Verhulst and Arjen Nijeboer cite the above research in their *Direct Democracy*.

And in his *When the People Speak*, James Fishkin gives us the example of Deliberative Polls—which consist of public deliberations on policy issues conducted among ordinary citizens who are representative of the larger population—held in Texas on energy choices, in which the percentage willing to pay more on their monthly utility bills in order to provide wind power to the whole community rose by about thirty points. And the percentage willing to pay more on their monthly bills in order to provide conservation efforts for the community (demand-side management) also rose about thirty points.

The notion that one would pay more on a monthly bill in order to subsidize the cost of windmills or in order to subsidize conservation efforts seems like an indication that individuals are willing to contribute to the broader public interest.

Still not convinced? You're right to be a skeptic! But see further below for more on the topic of experienced responsibility and cooperation theory.

13 By the way, deliberation does not mean the end of leadership. The temperaments of some individuals might make them more influential than others; but this does not necessarily remove the opportunity for others to express their opinion.

Deliberation does not mean the end of enforcement, neither. Regardless of considerations about human nature, it is better to give assurance to everyone that rules will be adhered to by everyone else. Tax payment enforcement, to keep with the same example, would be maintained under the proposed system. In this sense, enforcement is one of the facilitators of cooperation, which we will discuss further below.

14   Jared Diamond, *Guns Germs and Steel*

15   There seems to be a positive correlation between direct democracy and the reported happiness of citizens, which is one of the components of a good life.

According to a comparative study of Swiss cantons by Bruno Frey and Alois Stutzer, reported in their *Happiness and Economics*, other things being equal, there exists a positive correlation between people's happiness and the level of direct democracy. And "the positive effect of direct democracy on happiness applies to all income classes." Direct democracy can lead to more happiness in two ways. It can lead to laws that better reflect the citizens' wishes (outcome utility) and the opportunity to participate can itself be a source of happiness (procedural utility). Jos Verhulst and Arjen Nijeboer cite those results in their *Direct Democracy*.

16   In public life, politicians play this role. Similarly in economic life, as our communities

have grown, we could no longer walk across the street and barter chickens for wheat, we now needed food supply chains.

17 In the process of writing this very essay, feedback has been gathered from people living on three different continents.

18 It is not so easy to liberate ourselves from the bias in favor of the status quo. In his *On Liberty*, John Stuart Mill writes: "Yet it is as evident in itself, as any amount of argument can make it, that ages are no more infallible than individuals; every age having held many opinions which subsequent ages have deemed not only false but absurd; and it is as certain that many opinions, now general, will be rejected by future ages, as it is that many, once general, are rejected by the present." And in *Utilitarianism*, he adds: "The entire history of social improvement has been a series of transitions, by which one custom or institution after another, from being a supposed primary necessity of social existence, has passed into the rank of a universally stigmatized injustice and tyranny. So it has been

with the distinctions of slaves and freemen, nobles and serfs, patricians and plebians; and so it will be, and in part already is, with the aristocracies of colour, race, and sex."

Today for example, we take universal suffrage for granted. In the words of John Rawls, referencing Jack Pole's *Political Representation in England and the Origins of the American Republic:* "Perhaps the most obvious political inequality is the violation of the precept one person one vote. Yet until recent times most writers rejected equal universal suffrage. Indeed, persons were not regarded as the proper subjects of representation at all. Often it was interests that were to be represented, with Whig and Tory differing as to whether the interest of the rising middle class should be given a place alongside the landed and ecclesiastical interests. For others it is regions that are to be represented, or forms of culture, as when one speaks of the representation of the agricultural and urban elements of society. At the first sight, these kinds of representation appear unjust. How far they depart from the precept one person one vote is a measure of their abstract injustice, and indicates the strength of the countervailing reasons that must be forthcoming."

And a similar account may be made of the right of women to vote, the abolition of slavery, the emergence of constitutional democracies, etc. Neither Bernart nor Elizaveta (from the introduction) managed to liberate themselves from the shackles of the status quo. But can we?

19 Perhaps an organic state of public affairs in which new groups are constantly being born, then morph, and disintegrate

20 That is to say, many more talented individuals with constructive ideas may have the opportunity to express and implement those ideas.

In his *Considerations on Representative Government,* Mill affirms that "it is evident, that the only government which can fully satisfy all the exigencies of the social state, is one in which the whole people participate; that any participation, even in the smallest public function, is useful; that the participation should everywhere be as great as the general degree of improvement of the community will allow; and that nothing less can be ultimately desirable, than the admission of all to a share in the sovereign power of the state."

And he continues: "But since all cannot, in a community exceeding a single town, participate personally in any but some very minor portions of the public business, it follows that the ideal type of government must be representative."

We cannot but agree with the diagnosis that is proposed in this text. It portrays very accurately, indeed, the state of society at the time of its publication, in 1861. Our simple contention is that the days are rapidly approaching when the latter constraint is becoming less and less applicable.

Bibliography

Aliaga, C. (2006). *How is the time of women and men distributed in Europe?* Eurostat.

Ariely, D. (2010). *Predictably Irrational: The Hidden Forces that Shape our Decisions.* Harper Perennial.

Aristotle. (1992). *The Politics.* (T. A. Sinclair, Trans.) Penguin Classics.

Arrow, K. (1963). *Social Choice and Individual Values.* Yale University Press.

Australian Bureau of Statistics. (2006). *How Australians Use Their Time.*

Axelrod, R. (2006). *The Evolution of Cooperation.* Basic Books.

Ball, P. (2005). *Critical Mass: How One Thing Leads to Another.* Arrow Books.

Berne, E. (1964). *Games People Play: The Psychology of Human Relationships*. Ballantine Books.

Bismark, D. (2010). *Voter Verifiability and Public Verifiability.* Retrieved 2011, from Verifiable Electronic Voting: evoting.bismark.se

Chomsky, N. (2005). *Government in the Future*. Seven Stories Press.

Dawkins, R. (2006). *The Selfish Gene*. Oxford University Press.

De Gaulle, C. (2010). *Mémoires de guerre Tome 1, L'appel 1940-1942*. Pocket.

Diamond, J. (1999). *Guns, Germs, and Steel: The Fates of Human Societies*. W. W. Norton & Company.

Epicure. (2003). *Lettres et Maximes*. (O. Hamelin, & J. Salem, Trans.) Librio.

BIBLIOGRAPHY

Études et Documents du Conseil d'État. (2006). *Rapport Public: Sécurité Juridique et Complexité du Droit.*

Feld, L., & Savioz, M. (1997). *Direct Democracy Matters for Economic Performance: An Empirical Investigation.* Kyklos, 507–538.

Fishkin, J. (2011). *When the People Speak: Deliberative Democracy and Public Consultation.* Oxford University Press.

Frey, B. (1997). *A Constitution for Knaves Crowds out Civic Virtues.* The Economic Journal, 1043-1053.

Frey, B., & Stutzer, A. (2001). *Happiness and Economics: How the Economy and Institutions Affect Human Well-Being.* Princeton University Press.

Gibran, K. (1993). *Le Prophète.* Le Livre de Poche.

Gilbert, D. (2007). *Stumbling on Happiness.* Vintage.

Haidt, J. (2012). *The Righteous Mind: Why Good People are Divided by Politics and Religion.* Knopf Doubleday.

Hayek, F. (1945). *The Use of Knowledge in Society.* The American Economic Review, 519-530.

Hessel, S. (2010). *Indignez Vous!* Indigène Editions.

Howard, P. (2010). *Life Without Lawyers: Restoring Responsibility in America.* W. W. Norton & Company.

Jefferson, T. (1776). *United States Declaration of Independence.*

Kahneman, D. (2012). *Thinking, Fast and Slow.* Penguin Books.

Kant, E. (1993). *Fondements de la Métaphysique*

BIBLIOGRAPHY

des Mœurs. (V. Delbos, Trans.) Le Livre de Poche.

Kimball, M., & Willis, R. (2006). *Utility and Happiness*. University of Michigan.

Kirchgässner, G., Feld, L., & Savioz, M. (1999). *Die Direkte Demokratie: Modern, erfolgreich, entwicklungs- und exportfähig*. Vahlen, Franz.

Knight, F. (1935). *Economic Theory and Nationalism*. Allen & Unwin.

La Documentation Française. (2011). *Constitution Française du 4 Octobre 1958*.

Lincoln, A. (1862). *State of the Union Address*. Annual Message to Congress.

Locke, J. (1824). *Two Treatises of Government*. C. and J. Rivington.

Maalouf, A. (1988). *Samarcande*. Le Livre de Poche.

Machiavel. (2000). *Le Prince.* (M. Gaille-Nikodimov, Trans.) Le Livre de Poche.

Madison, J. (1787). *The Federalist No. 10: The Utility of the Union as a Safeguard Against Domestic Faction and Insurrection.* Daily Advertiser.

Madison, J. (1788). *The Federalist No. 63: The Senate.* Independent Journal.

Martin, D. (2006). *La France malade de ses lois.* Retrieved 2010, from Analyses économiques, politiques et philosophiques: danielmartin.eu

Mill, J. S. (2008). *On Liberty and Other Essays.* Oxford World's Classics.

Milton, J. (2006). *Areopagitica: A speech for the Liberty of Unlicensed Printing.* The Lawbook Exchange.

Montesquieu, C. d. (1862). *Esprit des Lois.* Librairie de Firmin Didot Frères, Fils et Cie.

BIBLIOGRAPHY

Montesquieu, C. d. (1799). *Oeuvres Complètes de Monstesquieu* (Vol. VII). J. Decker.

Parti de Gauche. (2012). *Le Contre-Budget.*

Pink, D. (2011). *Drive: The Surprising Truth About What Motivates Us.* Riverhead Trade.

Pinker, S. (2002). *The Blank Slate: The Modern Denial of Human Nature.* Penguin Books.

Platon. (2002). *La République.* (G. Leroux, Trans.) GF Flammarion.

Pole, J. (1966). *Political Representation in England and the Origins of the American Republic.* Macmillan.

Popper, K. (1966). *The Open Society and its Enemies* (Vol. I: The Spell of Plato). Princeton University Press.

Rawls, J. (1971). *A Theory of Justice.* Harvard University Press.

Rousseau, J.-J. (2002). *Du Contrat Social ou Principes du Droit Politique.* Université du Québec à Chicoutimi.

Sapolsky, R. (2004). *Why Zebras Don't Get Ulcers.* Henry Holt and Company.

Smith, A. (2012). *An Inquiry into the Nature and Causes of the Wealth of Nations.* Worldsworth Classics of World Literature.

Sun Tzu. (2003). *The Art of War.* (J. Minford, Trans.) Penguin Books.

Taleb, N. (2010). *The Black Swan: The Impact of the Highly Improbable.* Penguin Books.

Verhulst, J., & Nijeboer, A. (2007). *Direct Democracy: Facts and Arguments about the Introduction of Initiative and Referendum.* Democracy International.

Voltaire. (1991). *Candide ou l'Optimisme.* Classiques Hachette.

BIBLIOGRAPHY

Von Humboldt, W. (1969). *Limits of State Action (The Sphere and Duties of Government)*. Cambridge University Press.

Washington, G. (1789). *First Inaugural Address.*

Ce qui reste d'une cité, c'est le regard détaché
qu'aura posé sur elle un poète à moitié ivre.

Amin Maalouf, *Samarcande*

www.ingramcontent.com/pod-product-compliance
Lightning Source LLC
Chambersburg PA
CBHW031444040426
42444CB00007B/962